CW00523749

CAMBRIDGE LIBRARY

Books of enduring schola

Women's Writing

The later twentieth century saw a huge wave of academic interest in women's writing, which led to the rediscovery of neglected works from a wide range of genres, periods and languages. Many books that were immensely popular and influential in their own day are now studied again, both for their own sake and for what they reveal about the social, political and cultural conditions of their time. A pioneering resource in this area is Orlando: Women's Writing in the British Isles from the Beginnings to the Present (http://orlando.cambridge.org), which provides entries on authors' lives and writing careers, contextual material, timelines, sets of internal links, and bibliographies. Its editors have made a major contribution to the selection of the works reissued in this series within the Cambridge Library Collection, which focuses on non-fiction publications by women on a wide range of subjects from astronomy to biography, music to political economy, and education to prison reform.

The Morality of Marriage

Mona Caird (1854–1932) was a British novelist and early radical feminist social critic who insisted on maintaining her independence after marrying. Her 1888 article 'Marriage', in which she criticised marriage for limiting and subordinating women and called for equality between partners, sparked a furious controversy, and brought her widespread recognition. This volume, first published in 1897, contains a collection of Caird's feminist essays. She analyses the indignities marriage caused for women, both historically and contemporaneously, and advocates both equality in marriage (including in domestic duties) and women's economic independence. Caird also examines and criticises contemporary ideals of motherhood, discussing legislation and changes in social attitudes which would improve the lives of mothers. This volume presents a detailed account of controversial late-Victorian radical feminist views and criticisms. For more information on this author, see http://orlando.cambridge.org/public/svPeople?person_id=cairmo

Cambridge University Press has long been a pioneer in the reissuing of out-of-print titles from its own backlist, producing digital reprints of books that are still sought after by scholars and students but could not be reprinted economically using traditional technology. The Cambridge Library Collection extends this activity to a wider range of books which are still of importance to researchers and professionals, either for the source material they contain, or as landmarks in the history of their academic discipline.

Drawing from the world-renowned collections in the Cambridge University Library, and guided by the advice of experts in each subject area, Cambridge University Press is using state-of-the-art scanning machines in its own Printing House to capture the content of each book selected for inclusion. The files are processed to give a consistently clear, crisp image, and the books finished to the high quality standard for which the Press is recognised around the world. The latest print-on-demand technology ensures that the books will remain available indefinitely, and that orders for single or multiple copies can quickly be supplied.

The Cambridge Library Collection will bring back to life books of enduring scholarly value (including out-of-copyright works originally issued by other publishers) across a wide range of disciplines in the humanities and social sciences and in science and technology.

The Morality
of Marriage

*And Other Essays on the Status
and Destiny of Woman*

MONA CAIRD

CAMBRIDGE
UNIVERSITY PRESS

CAMBRIDGE UNIVERSITY PRESS

Cambridge, New York, Melbourne, Madrid, Cape Town, Singapore,
São Paolo, Delhi, Dubai, Tokyo, Mexico City

Published in the United States of America by Cambridge University Press, New York

www.cambridge.org
Information on this title: www.cambridge.org/9781108021999

© in this compilation Cambridge University Press 2010

This edition first published 1897
This digitally printed version 2010

ISBN 978-1-108-02199-9 Paperback

THE MORALITY OF MARRIAGE

THE

MORALITY OF MARRIAGE

AND OTHER ESSAYS ON THE STATUS
AND DESTINY OF WOMAN

BY

MONA CAIRD

"J'ai bien peur que cette nature ne soit elle-même qu'une première coutûme, comme la coutûme est une seconde nature."
—PASCAL.

LONDON
GEORGE REDWAY
1897

TO WOMEN

" In the name of your years of anguish,
 In the name of the curse and the stain,
 By the strength of your sorrow, I call you
 By the power of your pain."

CHARLOTTE STETSON.

CONTENTS

PART II

THE PATRIA POTESTAS

PART III

THE END OF THE PATRIARCHAL SYSTEM

MARRIAGE

PART I

THE PIONEER OF CIVILISATION

PART II

MARRIAGE BEFORE AND AFTER THE REFORMATION

PART III

THE LOT OF WOMAN UNDER THE RULE OF MAN

PART IV

A MORAL RENAISSANCE

THE FUTURE OF THE HOME

THE MORALITY OF MARRIAGE

PART I

MOTHERHOOD UNDER CONDITIONS OF DEPENDENCE

PART II

MARRIED LIFE, PRESENT AND FUTURE

PART III

CHILDREN OF THE FUTURE

A DEFENCE OF THE "WILD WOMEN"

PHASES OF HUMAN DEVELOPMENT

PART I

SUPPRESSION OF VARIANT TYPES

PART II

SONS OF BONDSWOMEN

PART III

THE TYRANNY OF INSTINCT

PART IV

THE HUMAN ELEMENT IN MAN

THE articles in this volume have been republished by the kind
permission of the respective Editors of the Reviews in which
they originally appeared: viz., the Editor of the *North American
Review*, of the *Westminister Review*, of the *Fortnightly Review*,
and of the *Nineteenth Century*.

INTRODUCTION

THE first of these articles was published in the August number of the *Westminster Review* for 1888. It was entitled "Marriage," and is here reprinted with additions and modifications. The last was published in the *Westminster Review* for January and February 1894, and is the last article in this volume.

It is extremely difficult to compile a volume of essays, written at different times, on the same subject, especially if that subject be controversial, without repeatedly insisting on the same fundamental points of the argument; for on those points the whole contention hangs. Each essay, being self-contained, is bound to dwell upon them more or less, since no sub-argument is of any final value unless the main ground of the doctrine be also stated. Certain repetitions which occur in this volume are therefore intentional, indeed, unavoidable. In writing on this question from time to time, I have been endeavouring to go over the whole field generally, and in particular, treating the matter mainly from the historical point of view, and as much as possible—considering the vastness of the subject and the number of its branches —in a condensed form.

The whole series will be found to bring evidence from all sides, to prove that the greatest evils of modern society had their origin, thousands of years ago, in the dominant abuse of patriarchal life: the custom of woman-purchase. The essays show that this system still persists in the present form of marriage and its traditions, and that these traditions are holding back the race from its best development. It is proved, moreover, that it is a mere popular fallacy to suppose that our present sex-relationship is a natural and immutable ordinance, there having been a long period during which the family was ruled by the mother, and its name and property handed down through her.

It will be clear to any reader of the articles that sentiments and standards, rather than legal machinery, are relied upon as a method of reform ; the law being regarded merely as the means of stereotyping the advance in sentiment when it is achieved ; accompanying, not preceding, the change of feeling.

Therefore, it is idle, from my point of view, to point out the disasters that would follow any serious legal change, although such change must eventually be the sign and seal of the altered standards, and of the consequently altered nature of civilised mankind. It might be proved up to the hilt that freer marriage laws, if passed immediately, would end in social disruption, without for a moment weakening one word of what has here been written. Indeed, he who shows the evils which exist under our present traditions, has only strengthened my argument. Our social evils have been produced by the relation of man to woman as that of possessor to possessed ; yet they are, strange to say, adduced by those who uphold the order, as reasons for preserving that relationship intact. These evils, we are assured, would make any change in marriage impracticable. This is arguing in a vicious circle indeed ; and if we applied the method to every other question, it is clear that *all* reforms would be impracticable.

Imagine a young family, consistently brought up to over‑eat themselves, and imagine this tendency encouraged by all the household arrangements, so that self‑control would be neither expected nor possible. The effects of such training, when the family grew up, would, however, force its rulers to adopt some sort of emergency measures to mitigate the disasters which their educational errors had caused. And the first thing which occurs to the average intelligence, in such a case, is to make a number of rules and regulations, by which it is fondly hoped that the offenders may be coerced into orderly conduct. And now imagine this mode of education pursued, not in a single family but throughout a whole society. The results would naturally be the same, on a larger scale. Food, and all affairs connected with it, would thenceforth become a matter for stringent legislation; not only notorious gormandisers, but also average over-eaters would be hedged round with sumptuary laws. One and all would be forced to submit their commissariat department to the care of the State, and perhaps of the Church; and any unchastened attempt to evade such supervision would be deemed immoral license, and the offenders would be banned by society.

Now, supposing some one should protest against this interference with a man's culinary arrangements, as an offence against his personal liberty, we may be very sure that all those who had most ardently supported the gormandising system would cry out in alarmed concert: "For heaven's sake refrain from interfering with the Structure of Society! Can you not see that you propose to give rein to Gluttony in all its most repulsive forms? Do you not perceive that freedom of choice regarding food would land us in moral chaos of the most appalling description?"

This is a rough parallel to the case of the marriage reform, and it will partly explain the extreme difficulty of answering questions on what is called the practical side of the matter.

I have endeavoured to show that the misdirection of the mighty forces of heredity, education, habit, which have brought us disaster, might have led us, (had they been directed wisely), and may still lead us, to victory. But this is obviously not the work of one generation, nor of one department of reform, and it is for this reason that the matter cannot be treated in that brisk, business-like manner that seems to be desired. It is not like a question of local government, or even of imperial government, where the issues, however important, deal with the machinery rather than with the elements of human life.

It will be seen in the following essays that the doctrine here upheld is one which has for its foundation, as I believe, the facts of history, sociology, heredity, and indeed all human experience, rightly understood. Paradoxical as it may sound, it is for that very reason supremely difficult to give a satisfactory answer when one is asked what one would substitute for the present form of marriage, a question often put, as if it could be answered in the same manner as, for instance, what one would substitute for big sleeves as a feature of dress, when those excrescences ceased to be esteemed. It is not a mere matter of putting one object in the place of another object, as one substitutes one block for another in a puzzle. In the life of a tree, the later stages are not *substitutes* for the earlier ones. The development is continuous and gradual, the flower being the culmination of the growing process. In the same way, human nature is in a state of development, and its institutions are the expressions of its stages of growth. No great and fundamental institution was ever put bodily into the place of a preceding one. The new one was absolutely non-existent at the time of those first movements of thought which ended by abolishing the earlier condition ; and had the final state of affairs been foreseen by the reformers of the era, it would have no more been possible to anticipate that state by legal enactment than it would be to cause a flower to appear on a tree which was just beginning to thrust forth its first young leaves. It would be, however, perfectly possible to train that young plant, of set purpose, in such a direction, and to place it in such soil, as to finally cause it to bring forth that flower which, for many generations, can bloom only in the imagination of a small minority.

It is that process of training to which I am trying to direct the efforts of all who believe that the present relation of the sexes is barbarous, and that the coercive system of marriage is in only too complete harmony with that barbarism. What we have to deal with is the sap and life-force which produces the growth.

It will now be seen why the ever-recurring question : —What would you substitute for the present marriage system?—cannot be answered in a sentence. The true answer is not single in its character, but manifold : it would lead the mind of the inquirer over the widest fields of history, of sociology, of science, of psychology ; it would take him back into a far and legendary past, wherein he would find disproof of many a cherished preconception which, in his wildest dreams, he had never doubted.

Nevertheless, legal reform, though a derivative matter, is a very important one. The first step that we may look for, in this direction, is the equalising of the divorce law for men and women, and some greater measure of justice as regards parental rights. Very much later will the modification of the coercive element be demanded, and this will follow from the decline of the present possessive and barbaric sentiment. In course of time, people will begin to resent State interference with their private affairs, and especially will they object to being forced to live with one another against their will. They will not regard this compulsion as " sacred." By the time they have arrived at this stage of feeling, they must of necessity take a new view of the relationship *per se.* Seeing that they no longer tolerate the situation *when enforced*, they would naturally think more seriously before entering upon it at all. Marriage without its spiritual sanction would be held intolerable, and if so, wherein lies the danger of dispensing with coercion ?

In a recent unsigned article in *The Spectator*, the writer, whose sex is unknown, gives a vivid picture of a woman's life under present conditions ; and if ever anyone wishes to know why many women have not written Shakespeare's plays (as it is generally quaintly expressed) or composed Mozart's symphonies, he has only to read this eloquent description. It is seldom, indeed, that we find so clear a realisation of the weary detail of domestic duties, of the unending petty responsibilities, the constant call "to give small decisions and settle minute emergencies." Yet this writer, apparently so full of insight, actually does not hesitate to doom women for ever, quite irrespective of their individual tastes and powers, to the eternal treadmill. He (or she) observes: "The carrying on of the race is so important a function as to more than justify the devotion of the half of mankind *to this end alone*" (italics mine). So long as men have the disposal of the lives of women, through the might of law and tradition, we shall continue to hear utterances of this kind. Men will make and women will echo them. It will continue to be taken for granted that the accident of sex shall alone be held sufficient to fix the destiny for life ; the ever-serviceable plea of "nature" being adduced in support of the doctrine.

It seems to be forgotten that "nature" indicates all sorts of things which civilised beings presume to ignore, and that if we followed her dictates, in all directions, we should return to our aboriginal caves in the rocks, and pick up a precarious subsistence by devouring such missionaries as a beneficent Providence might send for the replenishment of our stock-pot. Moreover, we should be landed in strange predicaments, were we to conclude that because Nature has given certain powers, she requires them to be used to the exclusion of all others. Nature has bestowed the gift of sleep, but she does not require us to sleep all day and all night. She has bestowed powers of locomotion, yet she does not show marked displeasure when we take an occasional rest. Nature has presented us with noses, yet we are scarcely called upon to cultivate the sense of smell to the detriment of our other faculties, or to wander eternally from flower to flower, like some uneasy olfactory spirit. Nature has provided food, without, one may suppose, intending that life should be one long dinner. She has given "hands, organs, dimensions, senses, affections, passions," without making the somewhat unreasonable demand that we shall spend our whole time in exercising each one of these powers to the exclusion of all the others. To infer that woman should devote herself solely to the cares of motherhood, on the mere ground that Nature has given her power to be a mother, is about as good logic as any of the above instances.

Nature clearly has indicated fatherhood to man as much as she has indicated motherhood to woman, and it is really difficult to see why a father should not be expected to devote himself wholly to domestic cares ; that is, if we are so very determined that one sex or the other shall be sacrificed *en masse*. As an aid, moreover, to the selection of the victim-sex, we must consider the fact that the actual production of the race is performed by women. Therefore, they have done at least half the work, even if every other burden connected with the children be taken off their shoulders. So that if nothing but a burnt-offering will satisfy our yearning to decide other people's duties for them, that burnt-offering should clearly be man. Even *then* his burden would be light compared with that which woman has borne for centuries. The following articles strongly insist upon the injury that this age-long burden has inflicted on the bearers of the race, and they point out that it must be expiated by that race, for whose production this awful sacrifice has been enforced. We are now reaping the consequences of the wrong that has been done to our mothers and grandmothers, and the more closely one studies sociology and observes life, the more obvious it becomes that man is called upon to suffer, inch by inch and pang by pang, for that which he has inflicted.

The miseries and inherent indignity of the position allotted to women are, strange to say, brought out with extraordinary clearness by those writers who attempt, in a jocose manner, to represent the absurdity of the woman's claim by reversing the present relations of the sexes. The man, in these skits, is always a down-trodden, poor-spirited creature, overwhelmed with petty cares of that kind which, when undertaken by women, are described as holy, but when performed by men are deemed ridiculous. We find the husband watching over the infant in its interesting but somewhat agitating stages of teething, convulsions, vaccination, measles, while, at the same time, he takes care that the lady, who is engaged in public work, shall have excellent but economical dinners, a well-kept wardrobe, a thorough immunity from petty interruptions of all kinds, and that at the end of her well-spent day, she shall be greeted on the threshold of her home by a smiling help-meet, arrayed in his best neck-tie and shirt-front, with moustaches arranged with that daintiness which his true man's nature has taught him never to neglect from the moment of his marriage. Disguising all signs of the day's long wrestle, this soothing creature adjusts himself to the other's mood, be it grave or gay.

Nor could the situation be rationally objected to by those men who have so often explained to their wives that nothing could be happier or holier. Do they not remember that "the hand that rocks the cradle rules the world"? Why then this masculine objection to rock the cradle? The average lot being, we are assured, the happiest in the end, no reasonable objection could be raised by man to a fate which holds out so *very* average a prospect. And then, as we are reminded, there are all the consolations of philosophy, the satisfaction of "doing one's duty in that state of life into which it shall please God to call us"—which is the reward of a docile following of this heaven-traced path.

In short, woman could scarcely find a more brilliant

advocate than the writer who proposes to himself to
reduce her to absurdity.

There is another argument which I am assured
weighs very seriously with a large number of people—
viz., the argument based on the assumption that woman
is, by inherent nature, physically weaker than man,
and that therefore she is bound to accept whatever
position man may assign to her. (I give the argument
almost word for word as it was stated to me). But for
sex-attraction, it is further urged, woman would " probably have been stamped out of existence, just as the
ancient Britons succumbed to the stronger races that
conquered them." I will not stop to exhaustively
enquire what would have been the fate of man and
society generally, had man elected to "stamp woman
out of existence." In that case, there would probably
have been no troublous problems to solve for either
sex ; no bitter wrongs to redress or pains to alleviate ;
so, perhaps, it is to be regretted that this stern measure
was never carried out. Seeing, however, that mere
exterminable feminine adjuncts are still permitted to
move in human society, we have to recognise the fact
that this compromise has been made with weakness,
and to admit that, short of the universal extermination
which was neglected by our ancestors, there is no way
of effectually convincing the female sex, thus weakly
spared, that they have not claims to rights and liberties,
as members of the human family, claims which no
amount of physical weakness can annihilate. Indeed,
in a society with the smallest pretensions to civilisation,
weakness ought rather to strengthen than to destroy
those claims on the justice of the community.

It is interesting to note that this argument of brute
force is generally brought in, late in the day, after more
ornate reasonings have come rather to grief ; and it
strikes quaintly on the ear which has been surfeited
with the familiar arguments based on sentiment, or

morality, or social expediency, or anything and everything except on might as distinct from right.

It would, indeed, clear the course satisfactorily if
opponents of woman's liberties would frankly take their
stand on this ground of brute force, rather than enlarge
so much on the blessedness of woman's sphere, and her
extraordinary heaven-implanted attachment to it, and
all pertaining to it—especially its limitations. Why
waste time in so many assurances of the charm of the
"sphere" and the woman's delight in it, if what is
really meant, in plain English, is: "You have got to
take whatever sphere we are pleased to give you, seeing
that our muscles are superior to yours. You may be
thankful, in fact, that you are allowed a sphere at all in
this world, since we might easily wipe you off the face
of it, if we felt so inclined. We spare you because you
possess for us a temporary allurement, and for thus
permitting you to draw breath, you ought to draw it in
perennial gratitude and obedience, and not to grumble
at the size and structure of the cage that we have
assigned to you—and a very pretty cage it is, with
a charming compartment dedicated to the handsomest
of you, who have pleased our fancy by your beauty and
feminine charm: a tastefully, nay, luxuriously appointed
compartment, with bars of the most expensive gilt, and
provided at great expense; with an elegant transparent
roof which permits the open sky to be seen, thus producing, in the happy inmates, a delightful illusion
of being in the outer air. It is really childish and
undignified—as every right-minded person is always
telling you—to try to bend and fracture the thickly
gilded bars of this charming domicile (made to order
of the best materials), so that we are incessantly called
off from important avocations to repair the injuries you
so peevishly inflict."

This, then, is the argument which seriously influences
the minds of many persons; an argument, therefore,

which must be met with equal seriousness—in so far as human frailty will permit. First of all, then, the argument of extermination. Granting for the moment that this wholesale massacre of a sex is a practical possibility, the somewhat perplexing complication arises: that before this event could take place, woman must herself produce her own exterminators—or, at any rate, the exterminators of her successors. An Exterminator who never had a mother is not yet known to science. The conditions of the whole problem prove singularly complex, on examination. For, if man could annihilate woman by brute force, woman could as easily annihilate all male infants if she chose, and so bring about, in a less direct manner, the same final result of extermination, only the other way round. It is idle to say that man could prevent this. No precautions would avail—except, indeed, that of taking the whole care of all male infants into his own hands, which would effectually destroy the "sphere" idea, and introduce a social state disastrously out of harmony with the views of those who believe that the patriarchal order of society is in accordance with all sacred and natural ordinances. It would be a curious and harassing condition of affairs, in which man would have to exert constant and wearing vigilance to prevent woman from breaking into the nurseries where he kept his male infants, and toma-hawking them, with hideous howls and war-cries! It is even to be feared that man, under such conditions of anxiety, would speedily become a nervous, haggard creature, unable, it might be, to rescue his innocents from the hordes of ferocious female Herods, who would stalk him when he took his walks abroad, accompanied by his prattling charges, and lie in constant watch for an opportunity to wipe those cherished ones from the face of the earth. Granted even, that by a system of armed escorts, and warders and vigilant cordons of watchmen, the disaster might be generally averted, yet it is clear that society would be in a chronic state of internal warfare, with outbreaks at intervals of massacres of women by men, and of retaliatory massacres of infants by women. In fact, had it ever come to such a conflict, the sexes would have waged a war of extermination like the Kilkenny cats, and the human affairs of this planet would have come to an abrupt end—very much to the advantage, perhaps, of certain groups ot worthier animals.

That, then, would have been the result in the case assumed, if we grant the assumption that woman was, by original and unalterable constitution, weaker than man. But this is an assumption open to dispute.[1] Physical strength depends on the mode of life and training rather than on the sex, as history has abundantly proved. Women have been found, in different eras and centuries, performing tasks requiring great strength, such as dragging cannon, carrying heavy weights (savage women do all the work of the tribe except hunting), tilling the soil, wrestling, fighting and so forth. Women have, alas ! figured as gladiators under Domitian. But for the cares involved in motherhood— cares to which man owes his survival to adult life— there is absolutely no reason to suppose that woman would have been at any physical disadvantage with man —as perhaps the enemies of the King of Dahomey's fierce amazons could sadly testify. It is certainly among Life's Little Ironies, that men who have been able to enslave women, only because of their maternal solicitude, should now, at the end of the Nineteenth Century, sternly point out to woman that she ought to cheerfully accept the sphere to which man consigns her, on the ground that he might have consigned her to the cold grave ! Does it not strike him, that had it ever been a case of war to the knife between the sexes, woman could, at any rate, even at her weakest, have forced man to

[1] See the following essays, especially " Marriage," pp. 67-70.

choose between leaving her unmolested, and total racial extinction ? So that, all things considered, it does not appear that woman exists exactly on sufferance, in this world of strife.

If there is an instinct which withholds the hand of the woman from slaughtering infants, there is (as the authors of the brute-force argument point out) an instinct that equally prevents men from murdering women—to any large extent.

But there is a further consideration which is touched upon in the following essays, and which also bears on the argument of physical force. It has hitherto been assumed that if the constitution of woman has not been developed to its utmost, at least it has not been actually injured or distorted. Yet this, too, is a pure assumption which there are excellent reasons for doubting. Indeed, evidence is rapidly accumulating which makes it almost impossible to deny that the feminine constitution has been disastrously injured during the long ages of patriarchal rule, and that this beloved " sphere " of woman, where she was thought so safe and happy, has, in fact, been a very seed-bed of disease and misery and wrong, whose horrors will perhaps never be fully realised until the whole system has shared the fate of its fellows, and is looked back upon as we look back upon the practice of *suttee* or of slavery, or the sacrifice of human victims to the gods of savage tribes.

" It is a trite experience," says the author of " Life to Woman," [1] " that the objects least likely to arrest human observation are those which are most frequently before our eyes—inconspicuous from their constant presence ; and just so in things moral, the errors or faults most difficult to recognise as such are those which are so familiar as no longer to attract attention ; or if perchance noticed, have been so long existent as to be esteemed simply a part of the course of Nature."

What John Stuart Mill saw so clearly about half a

[1] Ellis Ethelmer.

century ago is gradually and slowly coming to be recognised and proved, bit by bit, through observation and research directed to the subject.

"I consider it presumption," he says, "in anyone to pretend to decide what women are or are not, can or cannot be by natural constitution. They have always hitherto been kept, as far as regards spontaneous development, in so unnatural a state that their nature cannot but have been greatly distorted and disguised, and no one can safely pronounce that if women's nature were left to choose its direction as freely as men's, and if no artificial bent were attempted to be given to it except that required by the conditions of human society, and given to both sexes alike, there would be any material difference, or perhaps any difference at all, in the character and capacities which would unfold themselves."

I have said that the assumption of woman's original physical weakness is entirely unproved, and that evidence points the other way, while it also indicates that her constitution has been grievously injured by the conditions of her long captivity.

But now suppose that we accept the assumption for the moment, and grant the strange hypothesis that Nature produced, *ab initio*, a congenital invalid to be the mother of mankind. Let us suppose that Nature designed this frail being, doomed from birth to helplessness, for the severe task of providing the earth with inhabitants, a task from which she was to have no rest or respite during all the best years of her life, be her sufferings what they might. Supposing all this to be proved, is this weakness of woman really a reason for adding further to her misfortunes, for making the hard path of her life harder to tread? Is the fact that it is possible for a man to extinguish that flickering existence, a reason for treating its possessor with manifest unfairness, while the feeble life still endures? Is *that* the principle on which a civilised being acts in other relations of life? Is that how he would conduct himself to a child, or a disabled man? Is that the principle upon which social rights and liberties are bestowed? Do they fluctuate with the development or decline of the muscular system ? Are they heaped profusely upon our professional prize-fighters ; are they withdrawn after a railway accident or a disabling attack of gout ? Do our sedate citizens engage in competitive pugilistic contests, in order that the list of victors may be drawn up for the bestowal upon them of civic rights ? Is it necessary for a man to demonstrate his ability to knock down and trample upon his candidate for election as member of Parliament, in order to be permitted to register a vote in his favour at the polling-booth ?

If such were indeed the qualification for the suffrage, the House would present a most pathetic appearance on the opening day, after a general election, when members would limp to their seats supported by crutches, displaying bandaged heads, arms in slings, wooden legs, black eyes, and other evidences of the conflict by which the superior physical force of their constituents had been proved experimentally on their legislative bodies.

If rights and liberties are really to be held dependent on the possession of brute force, competitive tests of this kind would be unavoidable. Under such a *régime*, it is true, women, in their present physical condition, would doubtless have to acquiesce in the arrangements made for them by men ; but then, be it observed, *all* physical weakness, and not merely the physical weakness of woman, would suffer the same disabilities ; therefore, there would be no special and peculiar injustice directed against women merely on the ground of their sex. All weakness *qua* weakness would be deprived of liberty, not all women *qua* women. Might, in short, would be right, consistently and always—not merely on particular occasions, when a particular class of victims was to be singled out for suppression.

Nor could it be objected by those who adduce the brute-force argument, that women, in their turn, should use a parallel argument with regard to children, urging that since women are so much stronger than children, the latter might be consigned to any " sphere " that women might select, and that if they chose, for instance, to shut their infants up in bandboxes, or to stow them away in wardrobes and chests of drawers, there could be no cause for repining.   Might women not exterminate children altogether if they pleased ?

In the same way, a good case could be made out for consigning invalids to a " sphere," and the usual crushing reply could silence every querulous complaint on the part of the incarcerated : " Look here, you had better be content with your sphere !   Don't you see our biceps ? "

In short, the argument regarding brute-force comes to hopeless grief as soon as it is subjected to the slightest examination.   It starts with a popular fallacy ; but even if that fallacy be taken as fact, the argument fares no better—indeed, it fares, if anything, worse.   It implies a wholesale repudiation of all those principles of social rights and justice on which civilised as distinguished from savage communities, are founded.   It denies the very foundation of civilised life, and the principle of civilised law.   The latter is, at least, an attempt to supersede brute-force, and to give justice to weak and strong alike. It may not always do so, alas, but how are we to regard the argument which refers us back to the principles of savages, and the lawlessness of primitive communities, which, indeed, were hardly ever quite so lawless as all that ?

It is, indeed, difficult to understand how such an argument could be seriously contemplated by any one who did not, at the same time, advocate the destruction of all the rights and liberties which have been so slowly and painfully acquired, through ages of suffering and effort.   To show that the emancipation of women would be at once a sign and a safeguard of our national liberties is one of the main objects of these essays.

Perhaps the whole drift of the present volume might

be defined by saying that it is directed, in whole and in part, against that popular view which permits man to dictate to woman not only her duties, but her very thoughts and sentiments. It traces to that idea, and to the purchase system whence it springs, the very root of social misery. For the manifold evidences and indications of this truth, the reader must be referred to the essays themselves, as well as for the methods of re-direction of human progress, which alone can bring social regeneration.

THE EMANCIPATION OF THE FAMILY

PART I

EARLY HISTORY OF THE FAMILY

" Ne retirons rien à l'esprit humain ; supprimer est mauvais. Il faut reformer et transformer."—VICTOR HUGO.
" 'Tis inhuman to want faith in the power of education, since to meliorate is the law of nature."—EMERSON.

THERE is nothing that appears to be more trying to the " natural man" than to be asked to dethrone, for the moment, from his mind, the idols of that particular phase of society in which he lives, and to turn his eyes towards the great company of forgotten gods. It is so hard to realise that these grotesque images were, at one time, worshipped in fear and trembling, just as we now worship whatever image the power of the Age may have set up for our adoration. With our untutored ancestors, as with us, fear was the ruling motive of the worship; with them, as with us, sacrifice, human and animal, was the method of propitiation.[1]

[1] The idea of buying safety or benefit for oneself or the community by handing over some other being to bear the anger and the punishment of the gods, is one of the oldest that is to be found in human history. Man has, it would appear, imagined his gods as beings who were ready to reward human meanness and cruelty, if only they were provided with a liberal supply of victims and burnt-offerings for their altars. The life of the Greeks and Romans was literally built upon this notion, and we find it everywhere in the earlier ages of the world. The old custom of walling up a living being—sometimes an animal, sometimes a woman or child—into the fortifications of a city, in order that the city might stand and prosper, is familiar matter of history. The same is to be said of the sacrifices of the Druids, and of those Etruscan races who played so stupendous a part in the course of civilisation, through their early influence, both hereditary and didactic, upon the mistress and teacher of the world.

Nor did our Northern ancestors bring into their conquered territories any finer conception of the nature of the gods. The following

21

No doubt in all ages there has been a tendency to take the ruling ideas of the time as "natural" and eternal, and even to look upon social institutions as many of the Brazilian and Portuguese traders regard the Indian picture-writings on the granite rocks in the Amazon districts, as the works of God. On any objection being made to this theory, the triumphant

sentence is from Mallett's "Northern Antiquities":—"When they had once laid it down as a principle that the effusion of blood of these animals appeased the anger of the gods, and that their justice turned aside upon the victims those strokes which were destined for men, their great care then was for nothing more than to conciliate their favour by so easy a method . . . when they would ask any favour which they ardently wished for, or would deprecate some public calamity which they feared, the blood of animals was not deemed a price sufficient, but they began to shed that of men." The author goes on to state that at Upsala, every ninth year, grand sacrifices took place, which all attended and sent gifts to. They chose among prisoners of war, or among slaves, in time of peace, nine to be sacrificed. The chosen ones were treated with honour by all. Sometimes, in great emergencies, the people sacrificed their king as the highest price of divine favour. A king was burnt in Odin's honour to avert a great famine. The kings in turn did not spare their subjects, or their children. Hacon offered his son, to obtain a victory. "The ancient history of the North abounds in similar examples." The victim "was conducted towards the altar where the sacred fire kept burning day and night." In a large brass vessel the blood was received. The entrails were examined to read the will of the gods. Part of the blood was sprinkled on the people, on the images, and sacred grove. Sometimes the chosen person was thrown into a deep well in honour of *Goya*, or the Earth. If the victim went at once to the bottom, she received the sacrifice ; if the victim floated, she rejected it, and the body was hung up in a sacred forest. Near the temple of Upsala was such a place, called *Odin's Grove*, which was full of the bodies of men and animals. The priest always said in sacrificing victims. "I devote thee to Odin," or, "I devote thee to a good harvest." Feastings followed, and immoderate drinking. "Everyone drank, afterwards making some vow or prayer to the god whom they named."

The Indian tribes have the same idea in varying forms, an idea resembling the Jewish "sin-offering" and "scape-goat." Interesting particulars of the Indian custom will be found in the works of Elie Reclus, among other writers. The Indian Todas have an expiatory cow (of all strange beasts to choose for this tragic fate !) "They cut her throat, and drive her calf away into the mountains. The Gonds pass over their crimes . . . to certain denizens of the poultry-yard, and make them fly away into the jungle. In like manner the Badagas load a calf with the faults of question is returned, "And could not God make them?" which, as the narrator remarks,[1] of course settles the point.

Yet all history proves that society is in a state of perpetual motion, and that there is, perhaps, no set of ideas so fundamental that human beings have not somewhere, at some period of the world, lived in direct contradiction to them.

Were human ideas as fixed as we suppose, or instincts as immutable, progress would be an impossibility. Progress is to society what the development of mind and character is to the individual. It is, perhaps, man's nearest approach to creative experience. Still, it is not impossible to forego that experience. The cause of national inertia appears to be the restrictive effect of a religion, or a changeless order of ideas, which makes a spell-bound people, inaccessible to new views of life.[2]

Progress is not an automatic force which goes on working of its own initiative, in spite of all opposition and without individual effort. There is a disposition to look upon it in that light, and to see for ourselves no danger of crystallising, as other nations have crystallised before us, under the influence of fixed creeds. Confucius has spoken the word of enchantment which holds the Chinese millions under an unbroken spell : in this country and among English-speaking people, the thirst for material prosperity is making a gallant attempt to pronounce a similar incantation. It is, at least, not inconceivable that these mighty forces should prevail.

the defunct and his ancestors, and drive it with cudgels into the midst of the forest. . . . Upon the young bull . . ." sing the officiating priests, ". . . we lay the thousand and eight sins committed by Mada" (Mada being the dead woman), "and all the sins of her mother, and all the sins of her grandfather, and all the sins of her grandmother, of her great-grandfather, and of all her family." A fairly heavy burden for one young calf !

[1] "Travels on the Amazon," Wallace.
[2] See "Phases of Human Development," Part I., p. 201 *et seq.*

The struggle to acquire wealth tends to absorb the energies and thoughts. People are disposed to take things as they are, to get the best they can out of the existing order, for themselves and for their families, without caring much what that order may be, or how many it wounds and kills. The disabled are not in a condition to protest to any purpose; they are looked upon as embittered by ill-success: and, of course, the prosperous think they have no cause for complaint—injured though they be, and often in far more deadly fashion.

In order to realise how completely our notions of family ties are matters of the moment, historically considered, and not of eternity, it is necessary to become more or less familiar with the customs of our ancestors in remote ages.

Among primitive peoples, we find notions of right and wrong flatly contradicting not only our own ideas, but those of other tribes, sometimes contiguous; and on no subject have they been more at variance than on that of the relations of the sexes. The right that founds itself on might has had far less originally to do with these relations than has been generally supposed, although when once legal right and might became united, might at once took advantage of the situation. Now what greatly surprises most people who do not happen to have given attention to this subject, is that an increasing body of evidence points to the original organisation of the family *through the mother and not through the father.*[1] Thus we find, at the very outset, that something other than mere force was the director of the earliest human relations.

Modern research has made it more and more evident that the idea of kinship in primitive communities attached itself exclusively to the mother and her relatives, and that the father, at first, had no dominant

---

[1] " See Marriage," p. 70.

position in the family: an idea very startling to us, who are all more or less imbued with the sentiments attaching to the later or patriarchal system. Historically speaking, the notion of kinship through the father is a thing of yesterday.[1] The prevalence of the matriarchal system is not only attested by legends and national poems in nearly every country, but it still exists among some Malay and African and many Indian tribes, though it is fast dying out in Sumatra, under the influence of Islam, and through contact with Europeans. The male line is beginning to take the place of the female; the mother's power is declining. Still the *semando* or marriage places man and wife on equal terms, and each is protected by a contract made by the respective relatives.

Lippert declares himself to be convinced that the idea of an exclusively maternal kinship at one time extended over almost the whole earth.[2] M'Lennan says:[3] "We shall endeavour to show that the most ancient system in which the idea of blood relationship was embodied was a system of kinship through females only." Bachofen devotes himself to proving the same point. The matriarchal system was also believed to be in force among the Etruscan people, as evidenced by the inscriptions on their tombs.

Remnants of this social condition in Africa are exceedingly numerous, and in many cases it still exists intact. Lippert alludes to the case of the Balondas, a tribe on the Zambesi, of which Livingstone gives an astonished account. Among these people, the man, on marrying, is obliged to accompany his wife to her kraal, where he has to supply her with firewood, and must on no account undertake work for any other person, without her consent. In case of separation, the children belong, as

---

[1] "Primitive Family," Starcke.
[2] "Die Geschichte der Familie," Julius Lippert.
[3] "Primitive Marriage."

B

a matter of course, to the mother. A transitional form of this practice is found among many other tribes, the husband going to live for a year in the house of his bride. By this time, the custom is merely a survival, for the rule of the father is fully established ; the unmeaning habit of spending the first year in the woman's home showing the singular tenacity of the older idea. There are many instances of this incorporation of the son-in-law in the maternal household, where he was treated, in some cases, as a sort of slave. We are living under a slowly disintegrating patriarchal system, and we find it difficult to realise any condition of family life wherein its main sentiment is absolutely non-existent.

That this patriarchal arrangement is founded, as so many take for granted, in the very constitution of human nature, nobody who considers the facts of primitive life can continue to believe. Not " nature," apparently, but the mode of making a livelihood, determines whether the mother or the father shall hold the family or the group together. Agriculture was the women's industry ; the herding of cattle or hunting of wild animals that of men, who seem not to have meddled with husbandry until comparatively modern times. Agricultural tribes usually traced kinship through the mother, while those who tended flocks and herds had an agnatic system of relationship, counting it only through the father.

These facts have been brought into prominence by recent writers, but mention is made of them by Sir John Lubbock, among others, before attention had been specially turned to the subject. In his " Prehistoric Times," published in 1869, he says :

" Indeed, if there be two possible ways of doing a thing, we may be sure that some tribes will prefer one, and some the other. It seems natural to us that descent should go in the male line ; but there are very many tribes in which it is traced from the mother, not the father."

He goes on to state that in Tahiti neither father nor mother is the head of the family, but the son, the father being merely trustee for his son. In Australia, he continues, the son gives his name to the father; in New Zealand the youngest son succeeds to the property; and among the Wanyameuzi it goes not to the legitimate, but to the illegitimate children. There seems to be nothing in the eternal nature of sons or fathers, or wives or mothers, that determines their function in the tribe.[1]

Startling is the account given by Nachtigall (quoted

[1] Among the Nairs of India and many other of the hill-tribes, customs throwing light on this subject are recorded. A few sentences from the well-known French ethnologist, Elie Reclus, may be useful here as indications of what is known and accepted by experts in the matter :

"But we are not going to enumerate all the peoples and tribes, who in India and out of India, decree succession from uncle to nephew, or, in more archaic fashion, from mother to daughter" (see "Primitive Folk," pp. 174-75). "A man who should lose at once his son and his nephew . . . would be considered as wanting in natural affection if he manifested as much regret for his son as for his nephew, even if he had never seen this nephew. . . . As for the land, it is transmitted through women ; the mother bequeaths it to her eldest daughter, with the understanding that the latter may confide its management to her eldest brother, who will divide the produce between the members of the family.

"It is evil worse than death if the *matrimony* must be alienated, and there are but rare examples of it. Such a transfer is symbolised by the seller pouring a little pitcher of water, taken from the alienated land, over the hands of the buyer. As far as possible the aforesaid matrimony remains entire age after age."

Further on Reclus continues :

"One of these Nair princes has never assassinated him who barred his way to the throne. This fact has not failed to be noticed in India, where patronymic dynasties have continually been torn to pieces by internal dissensions, affording their subjects an example of brothers slaughtering brothers, sons rebelling against fathers, fathers poisoning or blinding their sons. A contrast easy to explain : paternal right calls up terrible ambitions, creates inequalities, extreme disparities between those who are nearest. The matriarchate is a law of equality, incites to neither hatred or jealousy, tends to tranquillity and peace, apportions equally, save that in some places it is to the advantage of the younger.

"Proud and haughty warrior though he be, the Nair cheerfully obeys his mother, assisted by his uncle, and seconded by his eldest sister ; the by Lippert [1]) of the robber tribes of the Sahara. The husband takes his bride to his own house for seven days, but after that she returns to her parents. When she speaks to him she turns away her face, and avoids mentioning his name. He loses his own name entirely, and is called the father of his wife's children. His wife's relations avoid speaking to him; if he is sitting among a company of men, and his father-in-law comes in, he rises hastily and goes away. The ingrained enmity between a mother-in-law and her daughter's husband is carried to painful lengths among the Kaffirs, where the latter will not so much as mention her name. This inimical attitude is regarded by Lippert, Bachofen, and others as pointing to an earlier age of mother-right, the resentment being caused by the encroachment on that right by the man. This feeling is probably mixed up with the resistance which the family used to offer, in earlier times, to the forcible carrying-off of its daughters by men of another tribe.

Thus we find a hereditary basis for the (no doubt) divinely instilled and profoundly natural repugnance of a man for his mother-in-law! This sentiment can claim the authority of centuries, and almost equal rank, as a primitive and sacred impulse of our nature, with the maternal instinct itself. Almost might we speak of it tenderly and mellifluously as " beautiful."

The survival of this custom of capture (as is well known) shows itself in the marriage rites of innumerable countries; a pretence of force on the part of the

trio manage the common property, and he who participates in it renders them an account of his exploits and achievements.

"The mother then reigns and governs, she has her eldest daughter for prime minister in the household, through whom all orders are transmitted to her little world. Formerly, in grand ceremonials, the reigning prince himself yielded precedence to his eldest daughter, and of course recognised still more humbly the priority of his mother, before whom he did not venture to seat himself until she had given him permission. Such was the rule from the palace to the humblest dwelling of a Nair."

[1] "Die Geschichte der Familie," p. 44.

bridegroom and unwillingness on that of the bride being as necessary a part of the ceremony as the giving of the ring among ourselves.

In the " Arabian Nights," the same pretence is exemplified. To neglect these details would be looked upon as " bad form." In one South American tribe, the couple run away together and return after three days. The well-bred mother of the bride, if she has any respect for herself, at once turns her back upon her son-in-law, and refuses to speak to him for a year. In all probability she has previously done all she could to bring about the match, but the customs of good society oblige her to behave in this manner, after the success of her efforts.[1]

The transitional stages of tribal life are most remarkable and puzzling, for the customs seem to have neither object nor consistency, and can only be explained by assuming the survival of an older social order. The idea seems to have been almost universal among primitive people, that a woman must be provided with *independent* property upon marriage. Originally, she remained at home, and shared in the goods of her own community, but as it became the custom for the wife to live in the husband's home, her relations provided her with what was called in Germany the *Gerade*, or woman's heirloom. Starcke speaks of it as the part of the common property set apart for inheritance by women, as the *Hergewäte* (weapons and armour) was the inheritance of the men.

The *Morgengabe* was the bridegroom's contribution to this provision for his wife. It consisted in " such horses, goats, and swine as go before the herdsman " (*vor dem Hirten gehen*). So it is written in the Saxon land law.[2] It is curious to notice that when the patriarchal order became established, this same *Gerade* (*Mitgift*) becomes

---

[1] Lippert, p. 49.

[2] The ancient custom of the herdsman *following* and not *leading* his charges is here exemplified.

the property of the husband, and the wife is expected to bring it as a dower. What was originally the safeguard of her independence thus becomes a tribute which she has to pay to her lord and master.

As was to be expected, the growth of patriarchal rule meant the gradual degradation of the position of women. It is not very easy to trace the transition from the matriarchal to the patriarchal rule, but we see, here and there, signs of the two systems working side by side. No doubt the custom of capturing women of other tribes, and the later purchase which grew out of this, were the first steps in the patriarchal direction. Nevertheless, in many cases, the fact of being purchased does not seem to have immediately abolished the rights which the woman enjoyed under the earlier form. Although these had really received their death-blow, they lingered on— as old ideas and habits will—long after the foundations of the new order had been securely laid. Slowly at first, but surely, this new practice of buying a wife led to a totally new mode of regarding the marital relationship, and, above all, it affected the idea of parenthood. Up to this time, as we have seen, the father was not regarded as having any particular connection with his children ; and certainly he had no position of command. Very often he did not know them at all. M'Lennan says that no Nair knows his own father, and every man looks upon his sister's children as his heirs.[1]

The distinctly paternal feeling is not an attribute of primitive man, and its development appears to depend on certain social conditions, which lead to a new set of associations, awakening, among other sentiments, the vanity of the man, who thinks that all the good qualities of his children are inherited from himself, while their faults he traces cheerfully to their mother.

For many centuries after the father had become head of the family—according to these new-fangled notions, which

---

[1] See Note 1, p. 27.

we have been tracing to their origin—and had become, at the same time, the owner of his wife, by right of purchase, he rested his claims upon the children solely on *the fact that the mother was his property*, not upon the fact of his fatherhood.

In the subsequent articles of this volume, I have endeavoured to show how all the other deeply-engrained social and family sentiments of modern life take their root and origin in this fact. That fatherhood *per se* has any claims is a purely " unnatural " idea, if by " natural " we imply that which most people understand by the word, viz., innate and aboriginal.[1]

That fatherhood has been regarded as a merely juridical relationship, even under patriarchal conditions, is proved by innumerable indications, direct and indirect. The old Jewish law, which obliged the brother-in-law to marry the widow and " raise up seed " to his

[1] It is amusing to contrast with all these facts of human history, the speeches of several illustrious opponents of the Custody of Infants Bill, 1886. Lord Salisbury is reported to have said that he was " old-fashioned enough to believe that by the law of nature and the law of God the father was the person who ought to have the care of his child," and that to act on the proposals of this Bill would be " to disregard rights held sacred from the beginning of our polity, and resting on far deeper foundations than most of those which we have deemed firmly established." Lord Bramwell thought that the proposed clause (which gave powers to the mother as well as to the father in the care and education of the children) " would really add another to the terrors of matrimony." " There might be nothing wrong in the husband's conduct, yet because his wife entertained different views from him as to the bringing-up of the children, he was to be subjected to the annoyance and expense of legal proceedings." Lord Bramwell had asked the opinion of a learned judge, who had as large an experience in his judicial capacity of matrimonial differences as any man, and his learned friend had said : " If two men ride on one horse, one must ride in front." It appeared to be a foregone conclusion who that " one " ought to be. Lord Bramwell also objected to the clause, on the ground that it might " require the court to make an order, the effect of which would be to transfer the control of the children, which the father now rightly possessed, to both father and mother. That would be a dual control of the most vicious kind." There is no evidence to show that anybody present saw the humour of the situation.

dead brother, is a case in point. The children born under these usages were considered as the sons of the dead man. There is a similar custom in India, called the *niyoga*, which permits the same practice during the life-time of the husband of a childless wife. It is entirely on that husband's behoof; for there is among these people, as among the Chinese and many other races, an intense anxiety to have a son who can perform for the father the rites of the dead. Among the Ossetes (according to Starcke), the children of successive marriages are all ascribed to the original husband, and they inherit his property. If a widow should live, in succession, with other men, her children are all legitimate; and in Assam, where widows may not marry again, their subsequent children are nevertheless free from any stigma, coming under the protection of the dead husband's name.[1]

Starcke speaks of the juridical character of fatherhood, " of which," he says, " we have given so many instances," and shows that it rested entirely on the fact of the purchase and possession of the mother. While she lived in a state of comparative freedom, the notion that any one but herself could make a claim to her children seems never to have entered into man's wildest dreams; it needed a civilised society to arrive at that culmination of injustice and inconsequence, which we now try to poetise and defend, as best we may, with cheap sentiment and an appeal to what we are pleased to call " Nature."

We have the most varied evidence respecting races

[1] Speaking of the children of a wife who was allowed to return to her home after she has borne a certain number (three or five, according to the tribe), Lippert says that the new patriarchal system is strikingly indicated by the fact that now the children remain with the father. "Sie gehören eben nicht mehr jener (the mother), sondern dem, der diese gekauft hat, so wie die Früchte dem gehören der den Baum gekauft." (They belong no longer to her (the mother), but to him, who has bought her, just as the fruit belongs to him who bought the tree).

in different climates and under varying conditions; at times even under apparently exactly the same conditions, as in Sumatra, where there are two forms of marriage, the one involving the male line of succession, the other the female. It is interesting to notice that in the first (implying the male line), the husband buys his wife; while, in the second, the woman's family buys her a husband, who has to leave his own home and go to that of his wife, where he is treated partly as a kinsman, partly as a slave. The acme of horror, from a masculine point of view, is reached among the Kooch tribe, where the husband is subject to his wife and mother-in-law.[1]

---

[1] The Etruscans, whose great antiquity gives to their customs such peculiar interest and significance, traced their descent through the mother.

On the subject of this mysterious race, which at one time possessed nearly the whole of Italy, there are many controversies, but good reasons are given for believing them to have had some common origin with the Eastern races of Asia Minor. Their customs, sports, games, dances are, by tradition, of Lydian descent; and among the Lydians, it is to be noted, the family was traced through the maternal, and not through the paternal line.

Everything, in fact, points to the widespread prevalence of this custom among ancient peoples.—See Dennis, "Cities of Etruria."

The fact that both the Etruscans and the Lydians traced relationship through the mother was considered by ethnologists as pointing strongly to the common origin of these races ; but the later discovery of the great prevalence of this custom of course deprives the coincidence of any particular significance.

Gell, the author of the "Topography of Rome," writes as follows :— "The Lycians and Caunians traced their families by descent from females (Herodotus) ; and it is not a little singular that the Etruscans (if we may judge of them by their sepulchral inscriptions where the name of the mother is usually mentioned) seem to have done the same. It is curious also that many of the Etruscan names have the feminine termination in a : as Porsenna, Vibenna, Mastenna, and others."

In civilisation this remarkable people seem to have reached astonishing heights ; and every monument that is newly disinterred gives fresh evidence, not only of their skill, but of their qualities of intellect. From them the Romans derived almost all their institutions. The Etruscans (who are believed by many to have been of the same race as the Celts) appear, strangely enough, to have possessed powers of intuition, of imagination, and a reputed faculty for second sight and divination,

We can gather from this and from other evidence, direct and indirect, in what manner our modern system became inaugurated. " Nature " has evidently been altogether left out of account in the arrangements of these singular people.

The same lack of obedience to her supposed dictates is exemplified in the two great systems of primitive marriage : exogamy and endogamy ; the one insisting upon marriage with women outside the tribe, the other as strenuously enjoining marriage within it.

Among the Circassians even the serfs are forbidden to marry one of the tribe. M'Lennan quotes from Bell's " Journal in Circassia " the incident of an unlucky steward or confidential agent of Bell's host, to whom the man had fled for protection. He had fallen in love with and married a woman of his own tribe, and had thus become liable to punishment. The incident brings before the mind a very singular condition of affairs from our so-called civilised point of view, for this man had been living " in a fraternity of thousands of persons between whom marriage was absolutely prohibited." This surely indicates a respect for " law and order " such as civilised man has scarcely dreamt of. Facts seem to point to a most unexpected conclusion regarding the position which the passional impulses take in many primitive groups. These latter, however, differ among themselves enormously in this respect, and general statements are therefore unsafe. Marriage appears, in many tribes, to be regarded as an affair of state rather than of attraction or impulse.

Offspring were deemed of enormous importance in the patriarchal age, for then the number of a man's children

which seem to place them in relation to the more stolid Romans very much as the Celtic races now stand to the Teutonic.

From the Etruscans, it may almost be said, the initiatory forces of all modern civilisation have been derived ; and thus we find that in this case also women, *par excellence*, have been the initiators of civilising movements ; while men under the Roman patriarchate have imitated and carried out the ideas which they received from outside.

and dependents marked his rank in the community; and there was, besides, a very strong feeling about having sons to carry on the name and to perform the rites of the dead. It was these considerations which appeared chiefly to provide the motive in primitive marriages.

No matter under what aspect uncivilised man is considered, he contradicts all preconceived notions as to his fundamental instincts, and their action on his life.[1] It is difficult to find any trait that is quite invariable. Sir John Lubbock gives some amusing instances of this fact. The Malays always sit down on speaking to a superior; the Todas of the Nilgherry Hills show respect by "raising the open hand to the face, resting the thumb on the bridge of the nose"; in another district it is good form to turn one's back on a person in sign of respect, " especially when speaking to him." According to Freycinet, " tears were recognised in the Sandwich Islands as a sign of happiness"; blushing is said to be unknown among the Brazilian Indians, but after long intercourse with Europeans, the weakness begins to appear.

As regards what is considered fitting and unfitting in the matter of clothing, of course there is no standard other than custom. Wallace tells us of the women of the Amazon districts who, in deference to European feelings, sometimes wore a few deprecatory garments; but when they did so, they used to feel that they were a sort of degenerate " new women," lost to those sentiments of delicacy and reserve which used to distinguish their mothers and grandmothers in bygone golden ages. Lubbock goes on to point out differences in the idea of virtue. " The Sichuana language," he says, " contains no expression for thanks; the Algonquin has no word for love; the Tinnè no word for beloved; mercy was with the North

---

[1] The almost incredible feats of Indian Fakirs, Yogis, of saints and ascetics in all ages make this fact abundantly clear; and no one who has observed the astonishing power, even in what might be called ordinary men and women, of a fixed idea and profound conviction, will be disposed to dispute it.

American Indians a mistake, and peace an evil; theft, says Catlin, they call ' capturing'; the first virtue is revenge. Cunning and deceit are also much admired." [1]

" Is a man to starve," said an African indignantly to Captain Burton, " while his sister has children whom she might sell ? " This remark is also quoted by Lubbock, as well as Müller's assertion that in Peru it was thought shocking for a woman to bear twins ; she was driven out of society, and the poor twins were given to the wild beasts. The writer concludes his account of these customs by saying : " I cannot indeed but think that the differences observable in savage tribes are even more remarkable than the similarities."

All this goes to prove the apparently fortuitous nature of human customs, and makes it at once easier and more difficult to understand how it is that certain developments of aboriginal notions have taken place in civilised societies, to the exclusion of others.

The custom of capturing women has doubtless been instrumental in bringing about the dominance of man under civilisation. The establishment of the patriarchal rule was also due to the fact of the temporary weakness and engrossing cares involved in motherhood ; so that whenever some variation in the life of a community occurred, tending to alter the balance in favour of masculine rule, that advantage would not be likely to be lost. A new custom would thus grow up and become fixed.

" Force first made conquest, and that conquest law."

Gradually, with the altered position of the woman in the family, the old reverence for the mother died out, and she was treated more and more as a chattel and a slave. In the earlier days, the husband had in many cases been subjected to the tyranny of his wife's family, and often of his wife's mother : he now had his revenge.

It is not in average human nature, as hitherto existing,

[1] "Prehistoric Times," Sir John Lubbock.

to possess and not to abuse absolute power. The history of woman, from the time of the general establishment of the rule of man, is tragic in the extreme. No one will ever know the worst of that tragedy, for a terrible silence hangs over it, as over the sufferings of all helpless and disfranchised classes. Adaptation, however, appears to be invariable among organic beings : it is indeed the condition of their survival. Were it not for the existence of this adaptive power, the sufferings of many peoples—the Jews for example—must have ended in their extermination. To this law must be referred the greater number of those characteristics which are said, often with mere parrot-like iteration, to belong—and by the fiat of Heaven—especially to women. That all mankind (including woman herself) should have acquiesced in injustice of this tremendous and wholesale kind is not, in reality, surprising, humanity being what it is. Injustice no longer seems unjust to most of us, after it has received the stamp of ages and the seal of custom.

The power of undisturbed association of ideas in creating a belief, and in lulling the objections of the reason and even of the heart, has never been sufficiently realised. In spite of the astounding evidence of history, few people are able to believe that human beings can be strongly influenced by anything short of standing armies and a body of police, the majority entirely forgetting that they themselves are living under the thrall of ideas, and that this subtle ubiquitous power directs the whole tenour of their lives.

When sacrifices of children were made to Moloch, it was necessary that the parents should offer them willingly, otherwise the gift was of no avail. " The parents stopped the cries of their children by fondling and kissing them, for the victim ought not to weep, and the sound of the complaint was drowned in the din of flutes and kettledrums. Mothers, according to Plutarch, stood by without tears or sobs ; if they wept or sobbed, they lost the honour of the sacrifice, and their children were sacrificed notwithstanding." [1] Such is the power of tradition ! Year after year, the great metal image, with its fierce internal fire, stretched out its arms, and mothers brought their children and delivered them over to the idol, in perfect silence.

As soon as the woman ceased to be protected by the force of ideas—as soon, that is to say, as she lost her position as head of the family—her downward path was certain. There was no sentiment of justice, on general grounds, among savages ; their conduct was actuated by custom exclusively. We find, therefore, that women have been subjected to cruel ill-treatment, not only among savages, but among civilised people. Our modern forms of cruelty are direct descendants of the customs of patriarchal ancestors. [2]

Capture-marriage seems, at one time, to have been very wide-spread, and its immediate descendant, marriage by purchase, became the practice among many endogamous tribes. Exogamy seems almost to imply marriage by capture. Writers do not appear to have agreed that there ever was a period of unlimited promiscuity. It is held by some, that there always existed a tendency to form into groups, with a woman as centre. Polyandry is regarded as an earlier practice than polygyny. Polyandry, in different forms, has been traced almost universally ; more often, perhaps, in what is called its higher stage, when the men who had one wife between them were all brothers. In that case, all her children were regarded as the offspring of the eldest brother.

---

[1] " Phœnicia," George Rawlinson.

[2] M'Lennan quotes Sir George Grey's account of Australian wooing, which brings home to us the kind of existence the women of these tribes lead. " Even supposing a woman to give no encouragement to her admirers, many plots are laid to carry her off, and in the encounters which result from these she is almost certain to receive some violent injury, for each of the combatants orders her to follow him, and, in the event of her refusing, throws a spear at her."

We find that even virtue and vice often change places. There are countries where parricide is described as " not a crime, but a custom"; there are others where the father, or, rather, the head of the family, is regarded almost as a god.[1]

Ideas of what is becoming and attractive also vary in such a manner as to lead one to despair of ever finding a rational philosophic theory of the beautiful. In Guinea the men have their skin ornamented with elaborate patterns, like a Morris wall-paper, and in the Deccan the women present an effective cutaneous appearance resembling flowered damask. They cut the designs on the flesh with as much heroism as the modern civilised woman pinches in her waist, or the civilised young man wears intolerable collars. In some cases there appears to be a sort of beginning of landscape art on the bodies of these devoted savages. The dread of pain seems to deter them not at all.

Among many races there is no fear of death, as, for instance, the Paraguays, the Feejeans, and the negroes of Dahomey. The Chinese seem to share this indifference, since among them, as is well known, a man condemned to be executed can buy a substitute.

Primitive notions of religion are only less remarkable than some modern ones. Savages often get angry with

[1] Among the Eastern Inoits of the Esquimaux race there is a strange custom that flatly contradicts our ideas of what is natural. When a member of the tribe is dying, or believed to be dying, the men construct a hut of blocks of snow, at some distance from the village, and provide it with skins, furs, water, and a lamp that will burn for a certain time. Then the sick person is taken there, and lays himself down on the rugs; and all his friends and relations come to visit him and converse with him for the last time. There are neither cries nor lamentations: the dying man gives his last directions, and the last farewells are spoken. Then the friends silently depart, one by one, and the last of the number closes the snow-hut with a block of snow.

What happens afterwards in that place of sepulture, how the breath of the living man and the flame of the lighted lamp both flicker out together, or one after the other, remains for ever a mystery.

their gods; indeed, even the Romans used at times to lose patience, and take to stoning the sacred images. The Nicobar Islanders put up scarecrows to frighten away the deity, and Burton once heard an old Esca woman, who was suffering from toothache, offer up the following prayer: "O Allah, may thy teeth ache like mine! O Allah, may thy gums be as sore as mine are now!"

That primitive people have no narrow preconceptions as to the personal appearance of their deities may be gathered from the fact, that " when the missionaries introduced a printing-press into Feejee, the heathen at once declared it to be a god."[1]

In short, we are forced either to ignore all that is now known about the primitive habits and ideas of mankind, or to resign ourselves to surrender any pet theory about "human nature" which we may happen to cherish. And having submitted to that painful sacrifice, we are rewarded by finding another belief in the place of the former one, which is, after all, more inspiring. We discover that "human nature" need not be a perpetual obstacle to change, to hope, and to progress, as we have hitherto persistently made it; but that it is the very instrument or material through which that change, that hope, and that progress may be achieved.

[1] "Prehistoric Times." (Quoted by Lubbock from Kotzebue.)

PART II

THE PATRIA POTESTAS

" The extension of the law of equal freedom to both sexes . . . being required by that first pre-requisite of greatest happiness, the law of equal freedom, such a concession is unquestionably right and good."—HERBERT SPENCER.

" Let us know how it is to be shown that the limits we have set to female activity are just the proper limits."—HERBERT SPENCER.

AT the time of the founding of Rome, the patriarchal system appears to have been fully established among the Latin races, with its accompanying sentiments regarding family life.[1] That system became stereotyped in the ancient codes. Romulus is said to have been the author of the marriage laws and the laws of parental authority. They can, at any rate, boast a hoary antiquity. It is remarkable how the idea of perpetual tutelage is still firmly rooted among us, in a modified form, and how all the popular ideas of woman's sphere and virtues are to be found in that singular system of ancient Rome, which made the wife as a daughter in her husband's house, and her children as her brothers and sisters. The *pater-familias* handed her over to the power of her husband, who then had the same rights of punishment—nay, of life and death, which the father had previously enjoyed. He might even sell her into slavery. The paternal power in its extreme form, after three centuries, was ratified in the Fourth Table of the Decemvirs. The

---

[1] Etruria supplied Rome with kings, councillors, religious rites and mysteries, civil ceremonies, regal attire (the royal purple is of reputed Etruscan origin) ; and, through a large colony that settled on the Aventine, a very considerable admixture of Etruscan blood. (See Note 1 to Part I., Emancipation of the Family, p. 33.

But as regards their family relationships, the Romans seem to have followed the usages of the Latins only.

Twelve Tables were regarded for ages as the epitome of wisdom. " The young learned them by heart ; the old held them as little short of sacred."

The wife could not inherit except for her husband, and " if the original title were deficient, she might be claimed, like other movables, by the use and possession of an entire year." She was, legally, not a person, but a thing.[1]

In modern times, one must go to the Russian peasantry for a complete analogue to this development of the *patria potestas*. " If you cannot thrash your wife, whom can you thrash ? " the head of the family demands indignantly. The marriage ceremony principally consists in the handing over by the father of his whip to the husband, with the advice to use it vigorously.[2]

In Rome the family (as is, of course, well known) was not what we understand by the word. It was a group of kinsmen held together by its head, the kinship being counted through the male line only. In the reign of Augustus, the laws Julia and Papia Poppæa were passed, which obliged fathers to provide their daughters with a dowry, and forbade them to prevent their marriage. Many other changes crept in, and at last the Emperor Justinian, in his reform of the whole body of Roman law, placed married and family life upon an entirely new footing. The husband lost his absolute control over his wife's dower, and in case of separation he had to restore it entire.

It has often been said that during the five purest centuries of Roman history divorce was unknown. It is not generally added, however, that during that time women used to poison their husbands in a manner that not even respect for the sacred institution would probably now prevail upon men to put up with. Moreover,

---

[1] See Lecky's "History of European Morals," Maine's "Ancient Law," &c., &c.

[2] " Impressions of Russia," Dr Georg Brandes.

as Sénancour points out, " it would be most awkward to attribute the degradation of manners to divorce ; otherwise we should have to attribute to Christianity the extreme degradation of manners of the later Empire."

In this era, women attained a degree of freedom which is cited as the cause of the extreme corruption and the decay of the imperial power. This explanation, if accepted, would oblige one to ignore all the influences which were, at that time, combining to destroy the moral vigour of the people ; the vastness of the Empire, open on all sides to attack; the tyrannical form of government, which subjected a whole nation to the caprices of emperors half-mad with the intoxication of power ; above all, the contact with the luxury and the vices of the East, where certainly it was not the freedom of women which had plunged the nations in corruption.

Niebuhr goes so far as to trace the beginnings of decay to the time of Hannibal. " No one," he says, " thought of the republic being in danger, and the danger, indeed, was yet far distant ; but the seeds of dissolution were nevertheless sown, and its symptoms were already beginning to become visible." [1]

The freedom of divorce and the independence of women in Imperial times, are thus made responsible for a condition of things which had already commenced in the time of Scipio ! On this rough-and-ready principle, it would be easy to find causes for anything. We have merely to select any two facts that happen to be contemporary, and boldly attribute one to the other ; (it is immaterial in which order they are placed).

The later Roman jurisprudence, inaugurated by Justinian, became singularly liberal in its treatment of women. In the time of Gaius, the system of perpetual tutelage fell entirely into discredit. The family rights remained nominally unimpaired. The family *lent*

---

[1] "Lectures on the History of Rome," Niebuhr, chap. lxxxi.

the wife to the husband, not relinquishing their claim. Thus the husband had no longer supreme power over his wife, since this was still held by the family, but the appointed guardians of the woman left her, to all intents and purposes, to do as she pleased. The old religious form of marriage, in which the couple eat *far* or rice together, as a symbol of mystical union, had fallen into disuse.

Confarreation (the religious form), *co-emption* (the civil form) had been the old rites of marriage. Now, a form of civil union, which had previously not been considered entirely reputable, came into more general favour. The stricter enactments were altered or evaded, for there was no longer a feeling among the people corresponding to the spirit of these old laws, which for so many centuries had been unfitting women for liberty, and the whole nation for the liberal institutions which the Emperor Justinian had attempted to bestow upon it. The corruptions which followed might be attributed more justly to the cramping tutelage under which women had been held, than to the liberty which they afterwards enjoyed, without preparation or experience, and at a time so unfortunate as that of a notoriously corrupt Imperial government.

triumph of Christianity, there was a reaction against this liberty which the Roman women had attained, and against the easy laws of divorce.

The dramatic incident of the penance of Fabiola, described by St Jerome, brings before us, in vivid form, the fact and nature of the changes which Christianity was bringing about in civil as well as in religious affairs. Fabiola, a vain and beautiful lady of the house of the Fabii, who had divorced her first husband and married a second time, was seized with remorse for her conduct, and undertook to do public penance at the Lateran Church. Clad in sack-cloth, with her hair sprinkled with ashes, she walked through the streets amidst a vast concourse of people, who had thronged to see the beautiful descendant of Fabius Maximus, fallen with passionate tears in the dust, before the shrine of the Golden Basilica.

This act is represented as having "made a violent breach in the civil law, and prepared its reform under the influence of the Popes. . . ."

Thus we may be present in imagination, at the very moment of separation between the ancient imperial civil polity and the new influences of the Church or Papacy. This incident in the life of a notable Roman lady, converted to the new faith, brings us to what may be called the watershed of the two systems of influence—imperial and pontifical. From this date onwards, the streams all flow, in spite of minor aberrations, in the same direction. The lie of the land has changed, and we have left the world of the ancients behind us for ever.[1] We now see woman under purely Christian influences.

[1] It is remarkable that at the next clearly-defined turning-point or crisis in the history of the Papacy, a woman should again figure as the *deus ex machina*. It may be worth while to recall the situation.

The great Pope Hildebrand (Gregory VII.) had lately entered upon his momentous struggle with corruption within the Church, and with an imperial enemy without ; "unwilling and sad," he is described at the moment of his strange and enthusiastic election to the Papal throne, at the Lateran Basilica in 1073. "Unwilling and sad Gregory may well have been on that eventful day, the turning-point in the history of the modern world." It is thus that W. S. Lilly speaks of the incident in an article in the *Contemporary Review* for August 1882. "The apostolic throne was to be his cross." Lilly quotes the Pope's own words in a letter to Duke Godfrey, written a few weeks after the election.

"We see what care surrounds us ; we feel how heavy is the burden laid upon us ; under which . . . our soul rather desires the peace of a dissolution in Christ than a life in the midst of such dangers. The consideration of the task imposed on us so harasses us that . . . our mind must needs sink beneath the greatness of our cares, so completely, through the agency of sin, does the whole world lie in the wicked one, that all men, and those more especially who bear rule in the Church, strive rather to disturb her, than . . . to defend and adorn her."

The encroachments of feudalism upon the hierarchy, the corruptions of the clergy, the intense opposition offered by them to Gregory's determination to enforce reform, are all dwelt upon in the article, as well as

It seemed obvious to the leaders of the early Christians that the liberty and the easy divorce then enjoyed by women were the causes of the corruption of Roman society of that age, and Christian teachers declared themselves against both.   When male reformers set

his famous decree, and the Council convened by him at Rome, whence this "trumpet-blast of no uncertain sound was sent by Gregory through-out Christendom."

In the midst of these internal tumults of the. Church, the reforming Pontiff had before him the tremendous task of defending it from the growing pretensions of the Empire, and of wresting from imperial and feudal hands the usurped privilege of investiture. It was during this critical epoch of the feud between Gregory and the Emperor Henry IV. that the Countess Matilda played her memorable and momentous part in the conflict. Curiously enough, this lady was the wife of one of the Emperor's chief followers—Godfrey, Duke of Lorraine. After his death, Matilda, left entirely unshackled in the administration of her Tuscan domain, was able "to give the Pontiff that unbounded support and entire devotion which constituted his chief earthly consolation." We hear of the Pope setting out for Germany "under the armed escort of the Countess Matilda," of his turning aside from his route "by the advice of Matilda," and returning to her mountain fastness of Canossa, where, as Bertholdus relates, he "spent his days and nights in prayer, imploring the Divine guidance at this difficult crisis." Again, when the crafty Henry had laid a plot "for seizing Gregory at Mantua . . . the vigilance of the great Countess foils the proposed treachery." In short, to her devotion in his cause, to her wisdom and counsels, Gregory VII. owed his ability to contend against the vast powers that were arrayed against him on all sides.

Lilly regards this conflict in the light in which doubtless the famous lady regarded it ; as a struggle between the powers of darkness and of light.

"But in truth the conflict was merely an acute phase of the great strife, carried on with ever-varying issues through the ages of the world's history, as in that microcosm, the heart of each individual man, of which human society is but a vastly magnified representation. The cause of Henry was the cause of man's lower nature. . . . The cause of Gregory was the cause of that higher law which has its sanctuary in the con-sciences of men."

Such was the principle for which the Countess Matilda contended. Whatever may be said regarding the Church in its moments of over-weening power, there can be little doubt that, at this particular crisis, it was of the utmost moment for human liberty and progress that the Church—the representative of spiritual as distinct from temporal in-terests—should not fall under the complete domination of the temporal powers. Had this calamity happened, the Church would have been used about fulfilling their vocation, they level their first attacks against women, for if anything is morally wrong, it is the custom to conclude that the fault must lie with this sex. Moreover, being legally disabled, they are not in a position to retaliate when thus accused. The bigotry of the early Christian teachers gave the first check to the tendency to freer institutions; the next was given by the fall of the Empire.

The conquering tribes brought with them their own laws and usages, their own patriarchal system; and thereupon commenced a process of compromise between the barbarian codes and Roman jurisprudence. According to Laboulaye, the *patria potestas* of the Romans and the *mundium* of the conquering tribes, although both representing the power of the chief, are quite distinct in character; the *mundium* being for purposes of protection for the " pupils," while the *patria potestas* was chiefly for the advantage of the father. Among the Germans, the wife and children were able to acquire a fortune and to spend it as they pleased, and the power of the father ceased when the child attained his majority. The daughter was released from the *mundium* on marriage, but she then passed under a still more rigid government, from which nothing could liberate her. In ancient history the woman has been under the power of the father; modern history shows her under that of the husband.

Laboulaye [1] is much puzzled by one peculiarity in the Salic law, which certainly cannot be accounted for except by assuming it to be a remnant of the matriarchal age. The Salic law, it is true, excludes women

as a resistless instrument of that feudal tyranny which was already threatening to become intolerable in its brutal oppressions. For this timely check to the overgrowth of feudal and imperial influence, we have to thank not only Gregory VII. but the Countess Matilda, "the foundress of the temporal power of the Papal See." (In these words is this remarkable woman justly described by Burgess in his work on the papal city).

[1] "Condition des Femmes." Laboulaye, chapitre xi.

so long as there are males to succeed to the *allod*, or tribal land; but when the deceased chief leaves no children, the father and mother succeed together; secondly the brothers and sisters, and then the *sister of the mother, in preference to the sister of the father*. The *brothers* of the father or mother are not mentioned. Quite inexplicable is this sudden and inconsequent exception to the leading idea of the Salic law, if we suppose it based exclusively on the patriarchal theory; but very familiar to the student of the matriarchal age is that choice of the *mother's* brother or sister for inheritance. This preference for the mother's sister occurs in the *lex Salica emendata* adopted by Charlemagne, and is said by authorities to be consistent with the manuscripts of Wolfenbuttel, Munich, and Fulda. Against these authorities and manuscripts, the attempts of savants in the last century to suppose an error in the texts, because they were unable to reconcile these incongruities in the law, seems somewhat audacious.[1] The Salic law, cries Laboulaye in despair, is full of inexplicable difficulties.

The habit of the German tribes of setting apart an inheritance for the bride was remarked by Tacitus. Something very nearly approaching settlements seems to have been made to a woman on marriage, and the Church adopted the Roman idea that a marriage was not legal without a dower. The *Morgengabe* or gift of the bridegroom, the day after the wedding, was almost universal among the northern tribes. So large was often the gift that Luitprand thought it necessary to restrict it to a quarter of the husband's property among the Lombards. The Burgundians, Lombards, Visigoths, Saxons, had different laws of succession and marriage; in some, the

---

[1] "Condition des Femmes." "J'ajoute que la loi Salique n'est point la seule coutûme barbare qui ait conservé des traces de cette preference des femmes dans le cas dont nous nous occupons ; la loi Ripuaire, par exemple." The Ripuary laws were, in almost all respects, similar to the Salic.

Roman law remained dominant, while in others, the old Germanic ideas had full play. Women were greatly respected, but they were still under tutelage. If they attempted to resist the authority of the husband, they were, according to some authors, " drowned in mud."

The canon law had a very profound influence upon matters of family life. It overcame the civil law in many instances. It opposed divorce with all its strength, and even looked askance at second marriage. Its position on this question was strictly logical. Marriage, being a sacrament, could not be broken in time or eternity. It is difficult to see how, on any other grounds, the theory of indissoluble marriage can be reasonably upheld. A union that is sacramental, sacred, indissoluble—except sometimes—has in it elements of the comic. The civil laws of the barbarians admitted divorce for murder, adultery, or magic. The German laws, unlike the old Roman codes, usually allowed the mother to be guardian to her children. This was recognised among the Bavarians, Burgundians, and Visigoths. No agnate could interfere with the fortune and education of the children.

It is humiliating to remember that in England, till within a short time ago, the mother's right to guardianship was not recognised at all; that the father could appoint another guardian, excluding her, and that even now the devoted efforts of many liberal-minded men and women have not succeeded in obtaining for the mother her full rights to her children.[1]

A significant fact, which does something to tone down the impression given by Tacitus of the almost religious veneration in which the German women were held, is that if one of them were carried off from her home, and during her exile had children, these children were regarded as belonging to her husband, on the ground that she was *in mundium*—that is, she was his property,

[1] Custody of Infants Bill, 1886. See succeeding article, pp. 56, 57 *et seq.*

honestly purchased, and consequently her children were his also.

Here we may note, once more, the ever-significant fact among ancient peoples, that (whether in the matriarchal or patriarchal era) there has prevailed one and one only idea as to the rights of parenthood, and that idea is : That the children belong absolutely *either to the mother, or to the owner of the mother*, whoever he may be, and quite irrespective of whether or not he happens also to be their father. The right to the children has always been *enjoyed by* or *derived from* their mother. There is nothing intermediate. Whenever we find the father enjoying legal rights over his children superior to those of the mother, we may know, without further proving, that his wife is his property, legally considered, and that he derives his parental privileges from her, exactly in the same way as the owner of a walnut tree derives his ownership of the walnuts from his rights in the tree.[1] Sentiment may gloss over the fact, but that fact remains. And the law makes it baldly evident. Yet ninety-nine out of a hundred persons, if questioned, would declare their approval of the father's dominant parental position, while indignantly denying, in the same breath, that the wife could be described as her husband's property and chattel.

In more or less modified forms, this patriarchal idea has ruled the family with little change—considering the vast changes that have taken place in other respects— to our own day. Feudalism only tended to confirm it. Thus we have arrived to-day at a sort of lop-sided condition : Society moving forward in certain directions, whilst its development is held back in others by immovable family relations.

[1] The point to be made clear is that paternal rights take their rise in the ownership of the mother, and not in the relationship to the children or the support which the father may afford them. These latter circumstances are now merely employed as a justification of the anomaly that she who bears the children is deprived of full rights regarding them.

PART III

THE END OF THE PATRIARCHAL SYSTEM

" In the case of women, each individual of the subject class is in a chronic state of bribery and intimidation combined, . . . if ever any system of privilege and enforced subjection had its yoke tightly rivetted on the necks of those who are kept down by it, this has."—JOHN STUART MILL.

ONE of the most striking features of modern life is the position which the individual takes as unit of society. In former days the family occupied that post. Yet this change was rendered half futile, because only *male* individuals were able to assume this independence. The woman must on no account be accepted as a free individual. Meanwhile, civilised communities were organised more and more on the individualistic basis, leaving the woman without the protection which she used to enjoy under the old group system, while refusing to give her the compensating advantages of the new order. She lost security without gaining freedom. She still suffered every sort of disability, legal and social; yet there was now no certainty of support, no absolute legal claim which would keep her safe from the rush and scramble of the modern world. It is obvious that in a struggle where many succumb even when suffering no artificial disabilities, the addition of these to the burden makes the handicap almost hopeless.

The woman, crippled by training and by inherited inaptitude for self-reliance, with adverse public opinion and stubborn prejudices, not only of others but in herself, to fight against; with a thousand inborn fears, instincts, longings; with a physical nature, trained for centuries to one sole end and purpose, and weakened for all others; dowered with exquisite sensibilities, unending capacity for pain—the woman of the nineteenth century finds the old shells and sheaths of a decaying patriarchal system drawn away from her; while at the same time she is exposed, or liable to be exposed, to the full blast of the competitive tempest in which modern life is passed, almost from the cradle to the grave. She sees her brothers going forth into the world with a thousand advantages, to her denied. For them a good education, encouragement in study, fostered talents, cherished opportunities; for them a good start in life, so far as lies in the power of parents to bestow, and on the father's death, the inheritance of the bulk of his property. For her, there is nothing but discouragement, opposition, eternal admonitions and reminders as to duty; while the fact is daily more borne in upon her that the one thing left to her, if she would not displease all her family and friends, is to marry, and so provide herself with a home and competence.

But into this necessity, (for it is scarcely less), the modern spirit of competition also enters. Thus the woman must struggle with other women for the sole means of livelihood that has hitherto been recognised as fitting for her sex; the family claims from her duty and obedience, as of old, but it expects her to provide for herself. On no account must she go out of her "sphere"; but she is by no means certain of finding that "sphere," though she be ever so willing to accept dictation as to her duties and sentiments. If she does achieve this end, or, rather, "sphere," she is still under a modified form of the old tutelage, as far as restraint goes, but she is now treated as an individual as regards responsibility. If she sins, she is punished; it is only in matters to her advantage that she remains *in mundium*. She must pay taxes, but she may not vote; she may be divorced for unfaithfulness, but she may not divorce.[1]

---

[1] She cannot divorce—that is to say, unless she can also prove what the law would admit as "cruelty" on the part of her husband.

In entering the marriage relation (ironically called a contract), she takes upon herself a tie infinitely more stringent, infinitely more imperious and extensive in its action than the bond into which the man enters. Yet here also, though less free, she is equally responsible— nay, really far more so; for what is a man's sin against the claims of marriage compared to the woman's, in popular estimation ? I do not contend that this injustice was absent from the old system, for in that also, although a *thing*, the woman was often punished as a *person ;* nevertheless the family felt bound to provide for and protect her. If she were carried off or injured, a *Wehrgeld* was charged to the offender, not, perhaps, so much on her account as for the sake of her value to the tribe ; but the *Wehrgeld* in some of the States was twice as high for a woman as for a man, as if with the object of giving her extra protection. If a woman had a griev- ance against anyone outside the family, one of the men was told off to fight with him, a duty which the woman occasionally performed for herself.[1]

There are some people who would not be sorry to see the patriarchal system restored in its entirety, believing that the best qualities of women will disappear if they become free in all the relations of life. It seems strange that anyone can regard freedom as unsuited to a human being worthy of the name. Still, the idea is at least logical ; it has an artistic unity, and gives room for argu- ment. But he who would uphold the present confused, patriarchal, individualistic, woman's-sphere-and-woman's- responsibility condition of things, has no principle of any kind to take his stand upon. He must simply be an echo of what exists around him, without the power of a genuine reactionary, or the foresight of a progressive thinker. It seems abundantly clear that she who is treated as a minor must, in justice, be provided for and protected as a minor. But if this be true, the swarms

[1] "Condition des Femmes."

of women earning their own living at ill-paid work are
an anomaly.

On the other hand, if the woman is to share in the
change which has reorganised society, if she is to be held
responsible for her actions, and expected to earn her living,
either by competing with others for a husband (according
to the more respected and popular system) or by some other
means, then, undeniably, she must be freed from every
possible disability. The monotonous, one-sided training
of the past has already loaded her with too many of
these ; she must be admitted, on equal terms, to the
banquet of life, and nothing—no matter how shocking
to our previous ideas—must be forbidden her. There is
no rational alternative.

The present condition indicates a mere confused stage
between two orders : the old and the new.

Meanwhile, the spirit of liberty among women is increasing rapidly, and as soon as an approach to economic
independence gives them the power to refuse, without
harsh penalty, the terms which men have hitherto been
able to dictate to them, in and out of marriage, we shall
have some just right to call ourselves a free people. It
is then that marriage—at present a mere mouldering
branch of the patriarchal tree—must alter its nature and
its form.

Few seem yet to have realised what the independence
of women would actually mean, and how absolutely our
present marriage hangs upon their subject condition. Those
who have opposed the smallest relaxation of the old laws,
who have resisted the education and progress of women,
were, from their own point of view, eminently wise ; for
upon the condition of tutelage hung many a cherished
belief, many a " sacred institution." It has been easy,
hitherto, to maintain stringent forms of marriage, because
the real brunt of it has been borne by women. Is it
conceivable that when there are, in good sooth, really
two to the marriage bargain, one of the parties to it will

consent to fetter herself by bonds which the other repudiates ? The " contract " can no longer remain unequal, when women have some say in the making of laws which they have to obey, and it remains to be seen how tight and irrevocable men will be willing to make the bond which they, too, must literally carry out. All men who are eloquent about the " sacred institution " will know that it rests upon them to sustain the sacredness which they will then, perhaps, talk less glibly about. They can no longer depute that office to their wives, together with the children and the cares of housekeeping. The " sacredness " which depends on restraints and punishments for its existence can then be fairly considered on its merits.

The " sacredness " which has hitherto hedged round family life can be clearly estimated when we remember the position which the married woman held, as regards her children, before the passing of the Custody of Infants Act in 1886. Before 1886 the father of a legitimate child was, as far as legal rights were concerned, its sole parent, " though the law imposes on the mother, under criminal and other penalties, liabilities and obligations almost equal to those of the father." [1]

The case is reported of a girl who applied to the court for permission to spend her holidays with her mother, the latter being separated from her husband for no fault of her own. The court refused, on the ground that the father's rights were sacred. " With these sacred rights the court has not interfered, and will not interfere." Only in the most extreme cases of cruelty to the child would these rights be set aside. The father, says Lord Chancellor Hardwicke, " is entitled to the care of his own children, by nature and by nurture." This view seemed eminently reasonable to august opponents of the bill, nor do we hear that their grammatical sensi-

[1] " The Infants' Act, 1886. A Record of a Three Years' Effort for Legislative Reform, with its Results."

bilities were offended. It is amusing to observe their horrified indignation at the bare thought of the father having to act with a guardian appointed by the mother, although the latter, according to law, might be *altogether excluded* from guardianship in favour of some one of her husband's appointment, and the utmost she could expect would be the privilege (in *her* case—in *his* the humiliation) of acting with another guardian.

Even to this day, the mother becomes sole guardian only when no other has been appointed by the father.

She can appoint a guardian to act after her own and her husband's death, but not to act *with* her husband (as he can appoint one or more to act with her) unless he is declared by the court to be unfit to have sole charge. Thus even this bill, fought for so devotedly by its friends, has been deprived of its principle of equality. The fifth clause is supposed to be a great triumph for the mother, because it empowers her, even while living with her husband, to apply to the court on any question regarding the custody of the children, or other important matters ; and the court is actually directed to have regard to the wishes " as well of the mother as of the father."

Our country is to be congratulated on this achievement, and on the liberality of our law, which discerned fully four years ago [1] that a child generally has two parents, and that one of them, though comparatively unimportant—even verging on the superfluous—might feel hurt if her existence and wishes were altogether ignored. Naturally, there is no necessity to allow this little politeness to interfere with rights more sacred, resting, as Lord Salisbury pointed out, " on far deeper foundations than most of those which we have deemed firmly established." This, at first sight, strikes awe, but the sense of the phrase, under analysis, seems to " softly and suddenly vanish away."

[1] This article was written in 1890.

Immense is the benefit which mothers enjoy under that Act of 1886, yet even now their position is subordinate. The woman who bears, suffers, risks her life, rears, trains, watches—of whom, indeed, public opinion *demands* these things ; she whose body and soul have been subjected to this terrible service, has still only secondary rights to her children. She must still take the small mercies of the law and be thankful. Indeed, she has reason to be, seeing that four years ago she had no rights at all.

Consider all this in conjunction with the tremendous rigour with which maternal duties are pressed upon a woman ; with the demand that she shall surrender to her children health, happiness, and all hope of self-development ; with the unbounded, merciless condemnation which is heaped upon her if she prove a neglectful or unenthusiastic mother. In short, so amazing, so overwhelming are the demands made upon the woman, and so meagre the rights granted to her, that the sense of the stupendous injustice is almost swallowed by the sense of the stupendous absurdity, and—as fortunately often happens in the study of English law and English opinion—the stress of indignant feeling finds timely relief in a burst of laughter.

Upon gigantic absurdities like these the sacredness of marriage has for centuries been resting. Father and mother are to share pleasantly between them the rights and duties of parenthood—the father having the rights, the mother the duties. No wonder there was opposition to the bill of 1886 ! They were dear privileges that it attacked.

If we could only realise how fundamental, in our traditions, is the old patriarchal feeling, we should then more clearly see that marriage, with its one-sided obligations, is not a thought-out rational system of sex relationship, but a lineal descendant of barbarian usages, cruel and absurd, even when the warlike condition of society gave them some colour of reason, revolting now to all ideas of human justice and of dignity. While the community in other directions has been moving and changing, in this matter it has remained inert. This is the last citadel of the less intelligent kind of conservatism, and it has been defended with the ferocity and jealousy with which one instinctively fights for a last hope.

History and science are rapidly undermining it, by removing those imaginary foundations in the "will of God" or the "ordinance of Nature" on which so many happy theories have been built.

Since the birth of the comparatively new science of sociology, the favourite satires of men against women lose their brilliancy; they sound stupid and ungenerous as the taunts of gaolers against their half-starved prisoners.

To bring the institution of the family up to date is among the next great tasks of progressive civilisation. So very far it has lagged behind, that this proposal sounds like a proposal to break up society altogether. So much the worse for society. We have abandoned *some* of the patriarchal rights; why do we not sweep from our State these remnants of a system which we repudiate utterly, as far as political questions are concerned, but whose influence we still keep warm at the very heart of our life, in the home, where the history of the coming generations is preparing?

The right of private contract is a right very dear to a liberty-loving people; yet in the most important matter of their lives, they have consented to forego it! So long as the idea holds that a husband or a wife must, in assuming that character, consent to subscribe to a set of conditions decided by some other persons— dead and gone for centuries—and that if these conditions are not assented to, honourable union (as society considers) is impossible, so long will freedom be lacking in the most important relation in life, so long will the right of private contract be denied.

Without irreverence for the Past, we must see that the time has fully come to throw off the tyranny of surviving superstitions which are holding us back, and causing a dislocated social condition, because in public matters, and for one sex, we are working on the principle of individual freedom and the right of private contract; while in all the relations of the family, and for the other sex, we are still moulding our life on the worst side of the old patriarchal idea, and denying the principle of private contract.

When domestic life has thus been brought into harmony with civilisation, we shall have passed through a bloodless revolution.

Then, and not till then, ought we to regard ourselves as having left behind us the shadows of the Dark Ages; then, and not till then, can the development of science and of education begin to take their full effect upon the race, for then only will the *whole* race be open to all the best influences of the age.   Hitherto we have been fostering in our midst a School of Superstition, to which we entrusted the task of fortifying the minds of the rising generation against all the knowledge which the contemporary schools of philosophy and science were laboriously endeavouring to promulgate.

Equal rights for the two sexes; the economic independence of women (hanging in a great measure on the progress of our industrial evolution); the establishment, rapid or gradual, as may prove desirable, of real freedom in the home—this at last would bring us to the end of the patriarchal system.

May we speed the parting guest!

MARRIAGE

PART I

THE PIONEER OF CIVILISATION

*" Now I could multiply witness upon witness . . . I could go back into the mythical teaching of the most ancient times, and show you how . . . that great Egyptian people, wisest then of nations, gave to their Spirit of Wisdom the form of a woman ; and into her hand for a symbol, the weaver's shuttle ; and how the name and form of that spirit adopted, believed, and obeyed by the Greeks, became that Athena of the olive-helm and cloudy shield, to whose faith you owe, down to this date, whatever you hold most precious in art, in literature, or in types of national virtue."—*RUSKIN, *"*Sesame and Lilies."*

THERE is no social philosophy, however logical and far-seeing on other points, which does not lapse into incoherence, as soon as it touches the subject of woman. The thinker abandons the laws of reasoning which he has obeyed until that fatal moment ; he forgets every principle of science previously present to his mind, and suddenly descends to a lower intellectual plane, making statements that any schoolboy might scorn. Our philosopher—once so strict in logical inference—takes the same view of women as certain Indian theologians took of the staple food of their country. "The Great Spirit," they said, "made all things, except the wild rice, but the wild rice came by chance."[1] Women are the wild rice of the modern philosophical world. They are treated as if they alone were exempt from the influences of natural selection, of the well-known effects upon organs and aptitudes of continued use or disuse —effects which every one has exemplified in his own life, which every profession proves, and which is freely acknowledged in the discussion of all questions except those in which woman forms an important element.

[1] Tylor's "Primitive Culture."

" As she was in the beginning, is now, and ever shall be . . ."

There is a strange irony in this binding of women to the evil results, in their own natures, of the restrictive injustice which they have suffered for generations. We chain up a dog to keep watch over our home ; we deny him freedom, and in some cases, alas ! even sufficient exercise to keep his limbs supple and his body in health. He becomes dull and spiritless, he is miserable and ill-looking, and if by any chance he is let loose, he gets into mischief and runs away. He has not been used to liberty or happiness, and he cannot stand it.

Humane people ask his master : " Why do you keep that dog always chained up ? "

" Oh ! he is accustomed to it ; he is suited for the chain ; when we set him free he runs wild."

So the dog is punished by chaining, for the misfortune of having been chained, till death releases him.

In the same way, we have subjected women for centuries to influences which called forth a particular set of activities; we have rigorously excluded (even punished) every other development of power ; and we have then insisted that the consequent overwrought instincts and adaptations of structure are, by a sort of compound interest, to go on adding to the distortions themselves, and at the same time to go on forming a more and more solid ground for preserving the restrictive system. We *chain*, because we *have chained*.[1] The dog must not be released, because his nature has adapted itself to the misfortune of captivity.

He has no revenge in his power ; he must live and die, and no one knows his wretchedness. But the woman takes her unconscious vengeance, for she enters into the inmost life of society. *She* can pay back the injury with interest. And so she does, item by item. Through her, in a great measure, marriage becomes what

[1] See note to " Children of the Future," page 153.

Milton calls " a drooping and disconsolate household captivity," and through her influence over children she is able
to keep going much physical weakness and disease which
might, with a little knowledge, be readily stamped out; she
is able to oppose new ideas by the early implanting of prejudice; in short, she can hold back the wheels of progress, and send into the world human beings likely to
wreck every attempt at social reorganisation that may be
made, whether it be made by men or by gods.[1]

[1] Gibbon, in speaking of the effect of continued bondage and contempt
upon a particular class, says that such conditions appear to degrade the
character and to have rendered them '' almost as incapable as they were
supposed to be of conceiving any generous sentiment, or of performing
any worthy action."
    Indeed, it needs no Gibbon to tell us this.   The effect upon the human
being of consistent discouragement and contempt can be studied daily, if
we care to open our eyes.
    A child can be made actually stupid by incessantly assuring him that
he is so, and nothing is easier than to deprive a person of the ability to
perform a task by surrounding him with a penetrating atmosphere of discouragement, and unbelief in the possibility of his achievement.   It is
true that, in the case of certain individuals, the contemptuous discouragement may have the effect of inciting to stronger effort.   But this can
scarcely be the case with a whole class, still less with a whole sex, for the
chances of breaking through the ramparts of human obstructiveness grow
less and less, in proportion to the largeness of the class which is suffering
the obstruction.   For example : Suppose, in a Protestant land, a bigoted
Roman Catholic family subjected to petty domestic persecution a member
converted to the Reformed Church.   His position would be extremely
unpleasant, without doubt ; but still he could always find support and
sympathy among his co-religionists, and could break through the thin
walls of his immediate surroundings, and find asylum from the intolerance
of his home in the outside world.   Public opinion would be with him.
    Take, again, the unlucky case of the son of wealthy parents, who in-
sisted that, as it was unnecessary for the young man to make his living,
it was his clear duty to remain at home by the fireside, playing chess
with his father in the evenings, soothing his mother's declining years
with pleasant chat about her neighbours, walking or driving with her in
the afternoons, making knitted mittens for his sisters, paying afternoon
calls, shopping, and writing innumerable letters to relations all over the
world, in order to explain to them how his interesting family was passing
its time.
    Suppose, in short, that this young man is required to make himself
generally useful and agreeable to everybody at every time, in forgetfulness

Seeing, then, that women are not a sort of human " wild rice," come by chance or special creation, no protest can be too strong against the unthinking use of the hackneyed arguments against their emancipation, arguments into which are packed an unmanageable host of begged questions.

Having made this protest, I propose to trace as carefully as is possible in the space of this and the three following articles (1) The part played by woman as the pioneer of civilisation; (2) the nature of her position in marriage and out of it, at the time of transition between mediæval and modern times; and (3) her position at the present day.

Through improved means of communication, and

of self and with untiring devotion to his appointed duties. If that young man failed to take the view of his duty insisted on by his parents, he would find no difficulty in refusing to comply with their demands. And he would find this facility, not by any means because the demands were preposterous, but because they were unusual. No parent, however angry, would be really heartbroken at the refusal of a son to dance attendance on the family at the domestic hearth, and the young man could refuse the office without feeling that he was dealing a real blow to affectionate and devoted relatives by so doing. After all, nobody really expects such conduct from a son, and therefore does not grieve if he acts otherwise.

But now take the case of a daughter in such a position. The scene instantly changes ! Could *she* refuse to dedicate herself to the family, without inflicting a real and deadly wound on the hearts of her parents ? Could *she* break through the prejudice of her home, and find friends, relatives, a whole public outside ready to support and approve her action ? So far from finding support, she would have the whole body of average people dead against her, as well as her own training, fears, and the self-distrust bred of years of education in the school of feminine submission.

Instead of her brother's frank and flat refusal to comply with preposterous demands, the woman has to wait, to use tact, compromise, subterfuge, perhaps ; to eat her heart out through years of fruitless efforts to gain a modicum of freedom without causing sorrow in the process. What miserable conflicts with tyrannous opinion, with selfish affection ; what reproaches, wounded feelings, and heartache all this involves, could be told by many a woman of to-day, who has known the bitterness of these years of slow decay ; of seeing her health, nerve, ability, hope, fretted to death in this cruel and baffling conflict with conditions which she is assured are only waiting to reward talent and determination !

facilities for learning, the swiftness with which social movements make way among modern communities has much increased. It is for this reason that any institution that now lags far behind quickly grows intolerable.

It was impossible that the demand of women for freedom should become a feature of modern life, without the marriage-relation, as at present understood, being called in question. Their claim for freedom included —whether all who made it so intended or not—a claim for a modified marriage.

In the preceding articles, its varying primitive forms have been glanced at. No one who has convinced himself of the facts thus set forth will be able to believe in the finality of any particular form. He will be forced to recognise that the relationship between the sexes holds intimate connection with other social conditions. He will see that the subjection of a sex which may be maintained while that sex is economically dependent, can never be permanently established after that disadvantage is removed. He will then be also forced to recognise that our present ideas regarding marriage are founded on the fact of the pecuniary dependence of women—a dependence which has been the result rather of human injustice than of any natural disabilities of woman.

The legends and traditions of all ages and peoples go to show, that even as regards physical strength, women are by no means aboriginally inferior to men.[1] How

---

[1] As for their personal valour, every reader of history knows that when occasion and opportunity concurred, women have shown themselves to possess this quality in the highest degree, and as rulers they have a brilliant record. It is difficult to find any country, principality, or city that has borne a great part in history which does not prove, on research, to have been founded, saved, or advanced in fortune by the influence of some remarkable woman. The history of Switzerland, for example, teems with instances of wise women rulers. Among these may be instanced the following :—The famous " Spinning Queen " Bertha, wife

the idea of their inferiority has arisen, in the face of so much evidence to the contrary, is not easy to understand. The notion is probably confined to those communities that we call civilised. It does not seem likely that savage tribes, whose hard work is done, and whose burdens are carried by their women, share this idea of the native physical weakness of the working half of their community. The King of Dahomey, whose most formidable regiment is composed of fierce Amazons, can scarcely regard women as inferior in respect to muscle of the King of Burgundy (then a Swiss principality), is remembered with reverence, and called by the French Swiss "Mother of our Liberties." Hadwig, wife of Burkhardt of Rhoetia, was celebrated for her valour, learning, beauty, and goodness. Queen Agnes of Königsfelder was called in as umpire to decide the differences between Duke Albrecht of Habsburg and the Perpetual League, "this wondrously shrewd and quick woman who had for thirty years swayed the Habsburg politics." The Lady Abbess of Zurich, the Duchess of Würtemberg, and many other notable women have assisted in establishing the fortunes and liberties of Switzerland.

As for the remarkable women of Roman history, especially in later times, when more liberty was enjoyed by this sex, their names occur incessantly, and it is a striking fact that in almost every case when the affairs of State were guided by a woman, the Empire entered upon a period of comparative prosperity, and its downward impetus was for the time perceptibly slackened. Gibbon, who has a sovereign and frequently expressed contempt for women, yet is bound to give testimony to this fact. In illustration of this disdain of the historian for all women, the following may be instanced:—He first describes the admirable and vigorous administration of the great Queen Zenobia, who raised Palmyra almost to the position of a rival of Rome ; he shows, moreover, that this had been accomplished at a time when the neighbouring states of Asia were sunk, one and all, in feebleness and corruption. Gibbon then adds : "Her sex alone rendered her an object of contempt." Not the most palpable and towering superiority could remove that eternal stigma of sex ! Gibbon quotes the saying of Tacitus regarding the ancient German tribes: "The Silures are sunk even below servitude ; they obey a woman."

The women of the Renaissance are of course proverbial for their brilliant learning and attainments, and many of the female saints enjoy a similar reputation. Catherine of Siena is perhaps the most widely celebrated among her sister martyrs. In the well-known picture at the Vatican St Catherine is represented as "appearing before the Emperor Maximilian, and carrying away by her knowledge a whole areopagus of philosohpers assembled to dispute with her."

and sinew, whatever he may think of their disposition. In Egypt, Spain, Germany, at different epochs, we have records which amply prove Dr Richardson's contention, that physical strength, in either sex, depends on the method of training in early life, and that there is nothing to prevent women, in the course of a few generations, from recovering the physical power which their mode of existence, and the ill-usage suffered during the long patriarchal ages, have combined to destroy. Even in one generation improved conditions and training can work miracles. The pressure under which women have lived, throughout these centuries of bondage, has been inconceivably great; indeed, until the burden is lifted, few will understand how crushing was its weight. So consistent and all-pervading has been the impact on body, mind, and character, that a uniform pressure has even been mistaken by many of the sufferers for no pressure at all, or rather for the inevitable misery entailed, as they believe, by existence itself. The absence of complaint among many women, of which we hear so much, often springs from sheer lack of experience of that sense of fresh, unrestricted, unfatigued power with which every human creature ought to start on the journey of life. To stand thus erect, with only the natural resistance of atmosphere and gravitation to offer a fulcrum for the living forces of the body and brain, this is what the women of civilised Christendom cannot hope to understand until they have learnt to realise that the unnecessary burden is not laid upon them by " Nature," but by their fellows.

Researches of recent years have brought to light the remarkable fact that woman, as the first agriculturist, the first herbalist, the initiator of the art of medicine, the discoverer of the most ancient of human lore, is, as Karl Pearson says, " the pioneer of all civilisation." So far from being the receptive and adaptive creature of popular imagination, she, in fact, holds the position of leader and originator in all the arts of industry: the prophetess and teacher of humanity from the beginning of its upward career.[1]

The transition from the matriarchal to the patriarchal

[1] Elie Reclus regards woman as the first architect. "Amongst our Hyperboreans, as amongst a great number of primitive people, such as the Tartars, and, for the most part, the negroes, the construction of dwellings is, as a matter of course, the business of women, who take the entire charge of it, from the foundation to the top, the husbands only assisting by bringing the materials to the scene of action. . . . I . . . see . . . in this an argument in favour of the hypothesis that woman was the first architect."

"It is to woman, I think, that mankind owes all that has made us men. Burdened with the children and the baggage, she erected a permanent cover to shelter the little family; . . . She laid there the fire-brand, from which she never parts, and the hut became illuminated, the hut was warmed, the hut sheltered a hearth. Has not Prometheus been called the Father of Men, to make us understand that humanity began with the use of fire? Now, whatever has been the origin of fire, it is certain that women have always been the guardians and preservers of this source of life."

Reclus goes on to show how the woman, rearing and taming some of the wild animals of the forest about her home—perhaps some fawn whose mother has been slain by the hunters—becomes the foundress of pastoral peoples.

"And this is not all . . . the woman . . . collected eggs, seeds, and roots. Of these seeds she made a store in her hut; a few that she let fall germinated close by, ripened, bore fruit. On seeing this she sowed others, and became the mother of agricultural peoples.

"In fact, among all uncivilised men, cultivation may be traced to the housewife. Notwithstanding the doctrine which holds sway at present, I maintain that woman was the creator of the primordial elements of civilisation."

In the times of the Empire, as Gibbon informs us, "all the linen and woollen manufactures . . . spinning, weaving, and dyeing were executed chiefly by women of servile condition for the use of the palace and army," and he mentions also "a gynecium or manufacture at Winchester." Thus the word *gynecium*—which implies that women are the workers employed—is used apparently as a synonym for *manufacture.*

Again, concerning the city of Carthage, Gibbon writes: "The picture of Carthage, as it flourished in the fourth and fifth centuries, is taken from the Expositio Totius Mundi. . . . I am surprised that the *politia* should not place either a mint or an arsenal at Carthage, but only a gynecium or female manufacture."—"Decline and Fall of the Roman Empire."

Though we hear so little about the lives of the poorer and servile classes of women in these Imperial times, there is little doubt that a system, as we have observed in the far Past, has created many anomalous ideas, as may be seen from the strange contradiction occurring in ancient myths and legends, as regards the estimation in which women were held, in bygone ages. As goddesses, as priestesses, as something powerful, mysterious, and sacred on the one hand! as things, as chattels, as temptations to sin, as necessary evils, as dependents, slaves, ministers of pleasure, play-things, child-bearers, on the other, have women been regarded in different eras.[1] It is not difficult, indeed, to find representatives of each and all of these views among

vast share of the real burden of all that magnificence fell on their shoulders.

Prophetesses, sibyls, witches are found in all lands and among all races of the earth. For instance, the responses of the Delphic oracle were given by a woman. Examples will occur in swarms to every reader.

Even the Moors had their prophetesses, as we learn at the time of their conflict in Africa with Belisarius, who (himself inspired, according to his own testimony, by the presence, counsels, and courage of his wife) went forth against a people who were led to battle by women. Under this command they held out against the Roman arms—and when Belisarius was the military commander—with astonishing persistence, and for a surprisingly long time.

In works of mercy it is seldom denied that women have been pre-eminent, but their power of initiation, even in these departments, is often disputed. Yet it is to a woman, Fabiola, the beautiful and penitent descendant of the race of the great Fabius, that we owe the foundation of the first regular hospital that the world has ever known. It was erected at Ostia at the expense and under the management of this lady in the early ages of Imperial Christianity (Wey's "Rome," p. 366).

[1] The Fathers of the Church are loud and unanimous in their opposition to feminine influence, in spite of the large and courageous part that women played in its creation during the ages of persecution. From beginning to end of its career the Church has owed to this sex more than can possibly be calculated (see note, p. 45, Emancipation of the Family, Part II.), yet it has consistently treated them with contempt and aided in their oppression. Accepting their bounty and support, it has ever delighted in their humiliation.

Its attitude is illustrated almost comically in the Church of *Sta Croce in Gerusalemme* in Rome, a *Basilica* founded by Helena, the mother of Constantine. She brought from Jerusalem a reputed piece of the True Cross, and built the Church as a noble casket for the relic. Now the Chapel of St Helena which holds this relic is divided into two halves by our civilised contemporaries. The incongruity is explained when we realise that the history of woman has been chequered even to the extent betrayed by these contradictory views ; that, at different epochs in her career, her " nature " has been regarded in all these varying lights, and that, in every case, that most astonishing " nature " has been supposed to be immutable, inherent, and divinely ordained from the beginning.

To condense the essential history of women after the introduction of patriarchal rule, into a sentence, we may say that woman originally became the property of man by right of capture ; now the wife is his by right of law.

Yet for many centuries we continue to see evident traces of the old age of mother-rule, Karl Pearson finding even in the witch-persecutions of the Middle Ages remnants of the old belief in the woman's mysterious power and knowledge, and of man's determination to extinguish it. The awe remained (according to this writer) in the form of superstition, but the old reverence was turned into antagonism. There was a struggle for supremacy between the sexes, and in early literature this struggle is evident, as well as the sentiment that women are all evil creatures, thirsting for unholy power, and must be resisted by all good and valiant men.

a grating, and this grating, so it is decreed, "women cannot pass without incurring excommunication." Women are thus excluded from the sanctuary of a chapel dedicated to a woman, in a church built by a woman, and forbidden to approach the sacred relic placed there by a woman, that relic being the very reason why the Basilica of Sta Croce in Gerusalemme has any existence.

The question almost suggests itself : was it done for a joke !

PART II

MARRIAGE BEFORE AND AFTER THE REFORMATION

" There is no sort of vexation which among civilised peoples man cannot inflict upon woman with impunity."—DIDEROT.

ON the spread of Christianity and the ascetic doctrines of its later teachers, feminine influence had received a severe check.[1] "Woman"! exclaims Tertullian with startling frankness, "thou art the gate of hell"! This is the key-note of the monastic age. Woman was an ally of Satan, striving to lead men away from the paths of righteousness. She appears to have succeeded very brilliantly! We have a century of almost universal chaos, ushering in the period of the minnesingers and the troubadours, or what is called the age of chivalry. Chaotic, however, as was this era, it brought forth some of the most beautiful conceptions of conduct which the human heart has ever created.

Perhaps it is idle to attempt to imagine what would have happened if some particular influence had been absent, at a particular historical juncture; yet it is difficult to avoid speculating as to the probable line of European development, if mediæval chivalry had not arisen to

[1] It is usual to trace all improvements in the position of women to Christianity. Whatever may be thought regarding the ultimate influence of this faith on social relations, its first effect was hostile to female interests. That is to say, it arrested the very marked movement that was going on under the influence of Justinian in the direction of bestowing greater freedom on women. This freedom was at once denounced by the Christian teachers as the cause of the corruptions of society. The agent of the devil let loose among men for their destruction : such was the early Christian estimate of woman. Lecky attributes their upward movement in the age of Justinian to the more mystical Oriental philosophies which had superseded Stoicism.

provide humanity with a set of ideals which, to this day, represent all that is generous and honourable in conduct, and all that is noble and courteous in manners. Nearly all writers agree in tracing to the romantic spirit of this institution, the development and fixing of those sentiments of reverence for weakness, and contempt for cowardly aggression, which tend to keep society healthy and possible, to this day. The spirit that we call chivalrous arose in an age of barbarism, almost like a miracle, for no really adequate cause appears to be traceable for its advent, in the midst of so much that was dark and brutal.[1]

Yet out of that darkness the beautiful conceptions of chivalry sprang into being, giving rights to the weak, demanding mercy from the strong, and founding the ideal of manliness on that of pity and of service. It is difficult to conceive an ideal more opposed to that of the Scandinavian ancestors of the Germanic peoples, among whom, nevertheless, chivalry took its rise. These fierce northern savages, who lived only to slay, looked upon mercy as another name for feebleness, and on service as degrading to the dignity of the warrior, who alone among men was worthy of respect.

It has been observed by thoughtful writers, that in the age of chivalry arose an entirely new sentiment, the sentiment of love as it is understood by modern civilised peoples; love, with an element of idealism and reverence, as distinguished from the passion as represented in all literature before the Middle Ages. Out of what unpromising soil this new flower of the spirit came forth

---

[1] "I am not sure that we could trace very minutely the condition of women for the period between the subversion of the Roman Empire and the first Crusade . . . there seems, however, to have been more roughness in the social intercourse between the sexes than we find at a later period."—Hallam, "Europe during the Middle Ages."

"Courtesy had always been the proper attribute of knighthood, protection of the weak its legitimate duty ; but these were heightened to a pitch of enthusiasm when woman became their object."—Hallam.

is perhaps most readily seen by recalling one of the elements of that feudal state, which yet must be given the credit of having produced it.

"The suzerain," says Guizot, "had also the right of marriage, that is to say, the right of offering a husband to the heiress of a fief, and of obliging her to choose among those offered to her. . . . The woman could only escape accepting one of the husbands, by paying the seigneur a sum equal to that which they had offered him to have her as a wife, for he who desired the hand of the inheritor of a fief, thus bought it of the suzerain."

When we see that such a custom existed at the time when the ideals of chivalry were coming into existence, we are forced to realise how enormous is the force of human sentiment, as distinguished from mere physical force, or even from fixed institutions. Chivalry not only bestowed upon the woman perfect freedom in the disposal of hand and heart, but required of the knight who should win her, devoted and lengthened service. It is, of course, easy to destroy the fairness of this picture, by dwelling upon a thousand points at which practice fell short of the exquisite theory. It is the beauty of the theory that is here insisted on, and its effects upon civilisation, to this day. Perhaps the fashion of sentiment has changed, for the moment, and the ideals of chivalry no longer excite enthusiastic admiration. At any rate, few people seem fully to realise how noble a type of character was actually developed during this age ; how fine a combination of qualities distinguished the best of the knights and the minnesingers. The songs and poetry of the latter are full of sweetness, and redolent of all the stirring romance that clings, for ever, to this era. With the quaint antique verses in which they celebrate their ladies and their love, many a picturesque scene of mediæval life seems to float back across the centuries, from grim, high-roofed, moss-stained German castles, such as perch, to this day, on the top of some inaccessible rock, looking down, in their loneliness, upon fields and plains at their foot, and dreaming—one might almost fancy—of the never-returning days, when the sounds of war and song used to fill the old halls with tumult, breaking the dead silence of the hill-top, which now broods there in mournful fashion, while it enhances the sadness and the beauty of these most convincing relics of a brilliant and generous era.

The stories of the vocal contests of the minnesingers in these old castles, before the counts and landgraves and their guests, have become part of familiar history. The very names of the minstrels carry with them a sweet savour from that epoch of gentle knighthood and "faire courtesie."

Walther von der Vogelweide, perhaps more than any other singer of his time, has this power of summoning back to us the epoch which he graced :—

"A man such as one would like to have for a friend, so bright in all his being, so gentle, for all his light and pleasing form, so inwardly earnest and firm ; merry with the gay, sad with the mourners ; full of hope from childhood on, and unwearying in striving after high goals ; fresh and cheerful even in time of need ; thankful for good fortune. Somewhat gloomy, indeed, in old age, and with good cause ; for spring and summer were over for the minnesingers, and Walther foresaw the approach of autumn."

Alas, the autumn that the troubadour foresaw for himself and his fellow-minstrels has overtaken his country and all the civilised world ! Sterner times were at hand for the merry land that he loved with so true a patriotism. Paradox though it seems, the Reformation was to sweep away all tolerance and urbanity from the war-tormented Empire, and Germany was no longer a fitting place for a man who had the assurance to assert that "Christians, Jews, and heathen serve one and the same God." [1]

The character of Martin Luther affords a singularly

[1] " History of Germany in the Middle Ages."—Ernest F. Henderson.

dramatic contrast to that of Walther von der Vogelweide, a type of the best outgrowth of German chivalry. Luther's influence served to modify, for ever, the effects of that institution, and to combine with other powerful influences of the Sixteenth Century, to initiate that particular condition of social life, which we may, broadly speaking, describe as modern, as distinguished from mediæval.

The great commercial development of this epoch, the increased navigation and discoveries of travellers, the growth of cities, and the sentiments which accompany wealth when divorced from mental cultivation, all played their part in producing the society of to-day, and the spirit that we call *bourgeois*. It was out of these materials that marriage, as at present interpreted, grew into definite form. It was at this time that immense stress began to be laid on outward sanctions, while sentiment and spiritual considerations of all kinds were increasingly ignored. This society became more staid and outwardly respectable. The obvious abuses of the chivalric era gradually lessened and disappeared; but the change can scarcely be regarded as indicating a genuine advance in moral perceptions. In fact, in some respects, it indicates a backward movement. With all the licence of the preceding age, sentiment and romance had been dominant; whereas, in the *bourgeois* age, a materialistic view begins to prevail. Forms and conventions are substituted for more romantic tests of right and wrong; the inward and spiritual is judged by outward and visible signs or labels; and in course of time, all question of the inward and spiritual has been forgotten, and attention becomes fixed exclusively on the labels. If the badge is satisfactory, its wearer is accredited without further question; if it be absent, or dubious, archangels may not hope for admission into respectable circles. Fortunately, there are few things in human fate that are wholly evil. This worship of mere form, this Apotheosis of the Label has doubtless had its uses in the training of mankind to obedience ; a blind and stupid sort of obedience, but still valuable as discipline, in the absence of a better kind of education. It may, perhaps, be compared to the drudgery of mere parrot-learning, which can never inspire the intelligence of the child, and often annihilates it, but may be of service—*faute de mieux*—in forcing the errant will to the discipline of application. Or, to regard the matter from a slightly different aspect, it may also be said that since the majority of mankind are not brilliantly intelligent, nor gifted with great moral insight, formal signs and labels must always be their safest guides, and that these alone can be trusted to keep them from straying into one knows not what bogs and quagmires. And this is true, so far as it goes ; only we must not forget that the same shepherding power over the multitudes can be claimed for *any* idols of wood or stone or custom, provided only that they possess a sufficiently terrifying aspect to scare their votaries into submission. A broomstick set on end might become a valuable civilising agent, if only the cultus of the broomstick could be brought to the point of commanding real terror. We may, in fact, be said to have ourselves reached that happy stage which might be impartially described as the Broomstick Era.

It is usual to take for granted that the institution of marriage, as at present interpreted, works in the direction of training mankind in self-control ; that, in fact, it is at once a terrifying and an elevating Broomstick. Yet the reformers of the Sixteenth Century preach a very different doctrine. They, in fact, teach the *impossibility* of self-control, *instead of its necessity*, and regard marriage *not* as a sacrament or a spiritual union, but merely as a concession to human weakness. Luther is most explicit on this point. Indeed, it is difficult to see how the Father of Evil himself, in his most inspired moments could have devised a means of placing marriage on a more degrading basis than that on which it was placed, of malice aforethought, by the great reformer. Those, in our day, who talk so much about the "sacredness" of marriage, can know but little about its history. Luther deprived it of all the spiritual significance which the Catholic Church had been so careful to emphasise, and reduced it to something little above a licensed sin. His celebrated sermon on matrimony leaves no doubt as to his point of view. It is, according to him, a necessary sin, which Heaven will forgive, because of the feeble nature of mankind. He lays enormous stress on the command to "increase and multiply," and obviously regards women simply and solely in relation to their powers of carrying out this exhortation. He hands over the whole sex—of course without consulting them in the matter—to a life-work which was, by his own showing, entirely physical; a work which doomed them to the existence of a docile and overworked animal, scarcely relieved by any other activities than those which might be expected to conduce to a more approved fulfilment of those duties.

And in all essentials, this is precisely the view that we hear reiterated in our own day by the orthodox, though their language, of course, is less "plain." Surely we need seek no more convincing proof than this, that time and familiarity will endear *anything* to humankind ! If marriage, as the reformers conceived it, be sacred, then nothing is profane ! [1]

Luther's doctrine was somewhat inconsistent as well as materialistic. For, while regarding marriage as a necessary sin, he also seems to regard it as a *duty*, condemning the celibate life with much acerbity, doubt- less through a spirit of opposition to the monastic

[1] "Abraham . . . believed God's word, wherein was promised him that from his unfruitful and as it were dead wife, Sarah, God would give him seed."—Martin Luther.

teachings of the Church. His views on this point have probably confirmed, if not exasperated, the perilous force of primitive passions. He has done much to hold back progress in particular directions.

Karl Pearson [1] takes a most uncompromising view of Luther's teaching, and sees apparently nothing but evil in the effects of the Reformation on the social relations. Bebel,[2] on the other hand, believes that its results were on the whole beneficial, chiefly, it appears, because Luther attacked the ascetic doctrines of the Church; while Lecky [3] says: "Protestantism, by purifying and dignifying marriage, conferred a great benefit upon women."

In this last utterance, may one not trace the influence upon the writer of those very doctrines whose enormous power over our own civilisation we have just been considering?

Lecky assumes, apparently as proved, that Protestantism dignified marriage; and it is difficult to avoid the inference, that he too has been taught to regard the prevalence of labels as trustworthy indications of a higher standard. It would, it is true, be difficult to show that society was really in a worse condition after the Reformation than immediately before it, nor is this task here attempted. But it is undeniable that the doctrine which influenced the relations of men and women at that epoch, was of a nature to degrade rather than to elevate those relations. If a better condition, nevertheless, followed this crisis, other influences must have been at work, and the improvement took place *in spite of*, and not in consequence of, the new doctrines. Other influences, in fact, *were* at work. This appears to be what Lecky has in his mind when he speaks of Protestantism having dignified marriage; for he goes on to draw a picture of the greater liberty of

[1] "Ethics of Free Thought." [2] "Woman."—Bebel.
[3] "History of European Morals."

thought and government, the general improvement and progress wherein marriage must, more or less, have shared.

In breaking the back of the ecclesiastical tyranny, Protestantism undoubtedly did one great service to women, for up to this time, their fate had been largely determined by the Canon law, which (as Lecky puts it) " has always treated them with signal injustice and contempt." [1]

Still, all improvements being allowed for, the woman's position, as established at this epoch, was one of great degradation. She could scarcely claim the status of a separate human being. She was without influence, from the dawn of life to its close, except such spurious kinds as could be stolen or snatched. The old chivalrous feeling for woman seems to have faded out with the romance of the Middle Ages. She figured as the legal property of man, the " safeguard against sin," the bearer of children *ad infinitum.*

Whether or not there was less real corruption than in earlier times, much real corruption now flourished under the cloak of respectability. Married life offered grand opportunities for tyrannical men ; for the general sentiment supported them in their tyranny, and sternly demanded absolute submission on the part of their wives. A man might indeed be a tyrant in his own home, in the devout belief that he was doing no more than exercising his just rights, nay, performing his bounden duties as ruler of the household.

Another striking characteristic of this epoch must be noted—viz., the concurrence of a more rigid marriage convention with the existence of a class of women who now (according to many writers) became organised, for

[1] See Note 1, page 73.

the first time, into a definite professional body, not unlike the trade-guilds which form so striking a feature of the period. The open corruptions of the preceding age were thus exchanged for a sort of orderly licence. The outcast class was formed into a strictly regulated band, subject to special laws, while the " honest " women were gathered into another fold and dedicated equally to the service of man, but under different conditions. They, too, were to wear out their lives in a bitter service, but this service, as their masters were pleased to consider, was suited beyond all others to the inborn " nature " of women—a service, in fact, that good women must regard as the most blessed and sacred ; epithets, by the way, which seem to be always employed when something peculiarly degrading is to be recommended, and when there really is absolutely nothing else that *can* be said to recommend it.

The whole social system thus built itself up, with order and decorum. The purity of society, about which there was much concern, was protected by punishing the delinquencies of the female half of it with extreme severity, in order, presumably, to make a good average of punishment, when taken in combination with the entire exemption from penalty enjoyed by the corresponding male offenders.

This arrangement was made easier by the growth of that professional class of women, who were at once imperiously demanded and sternly punished by the community, their offence being their response to the demand. This class, while obeying that social behest, without which they could never have existed, formed a convenient scapegoat on whom the penalties of transgression and the contempt of the virtuous could be freely showered, through whom, moreover, the sacredness of the home and the security of property, in duly wedded wives, could be thoroughly provided for. The arrangement was more than convenient. It secured from a

friendless class enormous services (or at least it secured
that which society demanded); it afforded the woman
who had become the legal property of one man, the
satisfaction of looking down on a position which she
was able to consider more despicable than her own—
wherefore, has never yet been explained—and thus
helped to reconcile her to social arrangements which
told so heavily against her.[1]

These despised women, who preferred, of the two
alternatives offered to them by society, the degradation
outside marriage to the slightly different and more
approved form of degradation within it, were, in many
cases, driven by misfortune and poverty to their lot;
the destruction of the nunneries, at the time of the
Reformation, having deprived many a lonely woman of
a place of refuge. Anyone who realises the conditions
of life at that time, cannot fail to understand what must
have been the fate of such unfriended women.

At best—or at what would be considered best—a
woman became the drudge and child-bearer of a man,
in " respectable " wedlock, wives being bought and sold
as if they were cattle, and educated at the same time,
with what can only be called ferocity, to do their "duty "
patiently, silently, devotedly, and to remain thus meek
and submissive under the severest provocation.[2]   Carried
off by the highest bidder, they were solemnly exhorted
to obedience and purity, to a life of God-fearing service,
and untiring devotion to their lords, in life and in death.
To drive a hard bargain and to sermonise one's victims
at the same time, is a feat distinctly of the Philistine
order.   Indeed, these well-to-do burghers, with their
commercial and practical instincts, were the true ancestors
of our modern Philistine, to whom they have handed
down, almost intact, their system of marriage and their
sentiments regarding women.

[1] See Note 1, p. 87.
[2] See Story of Griselda, of Marzia of Cesena, p. 204—etc., etc.

Bebel speaks of Luther as the interpreter of the
" healthy sensualism " of the Middle Ages. Any
" healthy sensualism," however, which did not make
itself legitimate according to Luther's ideas, was liable
to severe penalty, women offenders being subject to
truly terrible forms of punishment. But whether they
offended, or whether they conducted themselves according to the regulations, their lives appear to have been
hard and pitiful enough. Society was inventive as to
punishment, but showed little imagination as regards
rewards. Bebel says that —

" the married woman's duties were so manifold that a conscientious
housewife had to be at her post early in the morning till late at
night to fulfil them, and even then it was only possible to do so
with the help of her daughters. . . . Not only had she the usual
household cares of the modern housewife, but she had to spin,
weave, and bleach, to make all the linen clothes, to boil soap, to
make candles, and brew beer . . . to work in the fields and garden,
to attend to the poultry and cattle." [1]

Not indeed that hard work in itself is a grievance,
but *hard work without its rightful recompense of independence*—that is the definition of slavery.

At this time, history is strangely silent on the subject
of women and their occupation and status. Except
from accidental references, and what may be read
between the lines, it is difficult to gain an insight into
the real condition of the negligible half of humanity.
Their lives are to us a closed chapter, full of mystery ;
full, too, of moment, for silently and certainly, in those
obscure side-scenes of existence, all that we call modern
civilisation was growing into form : all the sentiments
and habits, even the very instincts that determine the
calibre of our present life, were shaping themselves,
with the unerring movements of crystal-atoms, as they
obey the strange internal impulses that drive them to
their inevitable devices. And thus, while women were
ignored in the obvious course of human affairs, and his-

[1] " Woman."—Bebel.

tory soared above their bowed heads, the material of that very history was forming under their hands.   In those shrouded homes, where the minds of children received their life-long stamp from the mothers of the race, all the determining elements of human sentiment were initiated and fashioned, in that mysterious process of spiritual crystallisation, which it is our habit to call Fate.

Meanwhile, the reformers were busy laying down rules, and proclaiming duties for the sex that is always expected to fall in pleasantly with any scheme of life which masculine philosophy may evolve—for " neglig-ible " though they be, it is clear that no social order could be carried out if women refused to bear their humble part therein.   And so, with loud voice and one accord, the reformers proclaimed that a woman's main duty and privilege was to bear children without limit ; that death and suffering were not to be considered for a moment, in the performance of this duty ; that for this end she had been created, and for this end—and the few others just enumerated—she must live and die. Even the gentle Melancthon, on this subject, says as follows :—" If a woman becomes weary of bearing children, that matters not : let her only die from bearing, she is there to do it."

Of course this doctrine is by no means obsolete.   It is the prevailing view of our most respectable classes ; those who hold the scales of public morality in their hands, and whose prerogative appears to be to judge, in order that they be not judged.   Remembering this, we cannot be surprised at Luther's teachings.   Why should a coarse-fibred monk of the Sixteenth Century consider sufferings which are overlooked by tender-hearted divines of the present era ?

As an instance of the way in which an exceptionally
good man of our own age can regard this subject—his
goodness notwithstanding—we may turn to the introduction, by Charles Kingsley, to Brook's *Fool of Quality*,
which Kingsley edited. A short account is given of
the life of Brook, who flourished (in a very literal sense)
at the time of the Restoration, and who was saved, as
his biographer points out in joy and thankfulness, from
the vices of that corrupt age, by an early marriage.
Kingsley goes on to describe the home where all that is
commendable and domestic reigned and prospered. He
dwells lovingly on that pleasant picture of simple joys
and happy cares, upon the swarms of beautiful children
who cluster round their father's knee, and help to rescue
him from the dangers of a licentious age. Kingsley
mentions, just in passing, that the young wife watches
the happy scene from a sofa, having become a confirmed
invalid from the number of children she has borne
during the few years of her married life. But what of
that? What of the anguish and weariness, what of the
thousand painful disabilities which that young woman
has suffered before her system yielded to the strain—
disabilities which she will have to bear to her life's
end? Has not the valuable Brook been saved from an
immoral life? (Of course, Brook could not be expected
to save himself!—we are not unreasonable.) Have not
Propriety and Respectability been propitiated? And
the price of all this? Merely the suffering and life-
long injury of one young woman, in a thoroughly
established and "natural" manner; nothing more.
Kingsley feels that it is cheap at the price. *Brook
is saved!* Hallelujah!

In order to understand how it happens that a good
man can think in this way without knowing his cruelty
(and that is the cruellest part of the matter!), it is
necessary to study the history of the Middle Ages and
the transition from that epoch to modern life. In that

study we shall come upon all the "forbears" of Charles
Kingsley's views, and realise that even good men
are the result of their antecedents, and that only in
special directions have our thinkers emancipated themselves from the thraldom of established prejudice.   And
it is for this reason that the progress of the world is so
slow : since even those to whom we have to look for
reform go on giving their support to all the old abuses,
except just those particular ones whose evil they have
themselves detected.   And so the world goes on, decade
after decade, with its needless miseries, its needless
wrongs, which the amiable and the distinguished conspire with the cruel and the selfish to perpetuate.
Year after year, women are ruined, in body and soul,
inside and outside the pale of society, the ruin in
both cases being essentially the same in nature, and
springing from the same cause.   A religious rite or a
legal form is, for a woman, to mark the whole difference
between irredeemable sin and absolute duty.   From this
significant fact it is easy to infer the nature of the
married woman's position, and to see that—unless
human laws have some supernatural power of sanctifica-
tion—her position is, *per se*, degrading.[1]   Women resent
this assertion, not unnaturally, since most of them have
to accept the position as it stands.   Yet nothing is
gained by blinking the fact, and much is lost by this
refusal to look matters squarely in the face.

Female education has indeed been devised to discourage any such boldness.   If women had not been
trained to regard facts as more or less improper—especially facts that affect themselves—society would be, at
this moment, many centuries further forward on its path
of progress.

From the system of purchase—which has been shewn

---

[1] It is of course merely the abstract status of marriage in its legal and
social aspects which is here alluded to, and not marriage as it may be
and often is.   See *Married Life, Present and Future*, p. 138.

to be the real foundation of our marriage system—arose our strange and inconsequent ideas of " honour " for man and woman. How many have realised that " honour " or " virtue " in a woman did not originally take its rise from any sense of personal self-respect, but from the fact of her position as the property of her husband ? This is assuredly no attempt to undervalue the quality itself, but to point out that the woman has actually been forced to develop her moral standards, not under the guidance of her own individual conscience, but *in accordance with the conditions of her servitude to man.* Just as a pointer acquires his peculiar powers through hereditary adaptation to his master's convenience, so, in very fact, women have acquired certain qualities, and, above all, certain standards of conduct, through hereditary training in *their* master's service. Undoubtedly, by this means, valuable qualities have been acquired (the pointer can boast no less). But it is not a little significant that they have been acquired exactly in the same way as traits useful to man have been acquired by domesticated animals. Thus women's virtues are not absolute but *relative :* relative, that is, to man.

A little thought will show how this is now, and has been, since the days of the patriarchate, the one standard by which female virtues take their measure.

It is thus, in fact, that the woman's chastity became the watch-dog of the man's possession ; it is thus that the dual moral standard for the two sexes has arisen. *The woman must protect the man's property in herself,* and failure in this duty is held as an unpardonable offence against the holder of the property.[1] To ask the man to

---

[1] There is a significant parallel to this attitude of mind in the story of the African slave, who, having been thrown into a river by a captious friend, broke out into furious imprecations, and ended with the culminating outburst : " You dam' blackguard—you see what you do ! You drown massa's black nigger ! "

develop the same quality that he demands in the woman seems to the vast majority, even now, very much as if some upstart " new " pointer should suddenly shoulder the gun and expect the sportsman to point the game !

The ugliness of all this, and of the facts on which it depends, is not the fault of those who *perceive* it, but of those who created it, and who now uphold it ; a distinction which the justice of the British public is not always ready to admit.

The ugliness, indeed, is largely modified by many overgrowths of nobler sentiment and chivalrous custom. Nevertheless, the origin of woman's virtue is very obvious to all careful observers, in the attitude of the public mind on this subject. The idea that a man's honour can be injured by his wife's infidelity is indeed a most naïve proclamation of the theory of proprietorship. It can be explained on no other assumption. Like many other incongruous ideas, this barbaric view of the marriage relation has grown into the very fibre of human existence, and has become associated with its closest affections. It is for this reason that its hold on mankind is so powerful, although it would puzzle most people to give an account of their faith that would be worth a second's consideration.

Probably few persons, whose attention had not previously been warned, would feel any shock of surprise or disgust in reading the following sentence from Lord Shaftesbury's " Characteristicks," a work bearing the date 1714.

The author is speaking of love-affairs in cases where the woman is married, and he describes the lovers in

And, in the same way, when the predatory lover prowls round, and seeks to lure away an indignant and well-trained wife, she exclaims in effect, though in far superior words : " You dam' scoundrel ! you see what you do—you want to carry away massa's white wife ! " (*e.g.*, " Sir, you insult me ! What right have I ever given you to suppose that I should be lax in protecting my husband's honour ? Would you betray his trust in you ? Leave me, sir ! ").

F

such cases as "Pretenders who, through this plea of irresistible necessity, make bold with what is another's . . . but the law makes bold with them in its turn, as with other invaders of property."

It is doubtful whether this very bald and frank description of the wife as "property" would startle an assembly of the orthodox. Why, indeed, should it, since that is, after all, precisely their own unformulated view of the matter ? When some divorce case makes the British public double its consumption of newspapers and express itself in horror and surprise, it is *au fond*, the invasion of property that causes the consternation.

The husband feels, in some mystic fashion, dishonoured by his loss, albeit it is the wife and not he who, on his own showing, has committed the crime.

Is it possible to be really dishonoured by any action except one's own ? One may be pained, injured, thrown into despair by another person; but, in the name of reason, how dishonoured ? Obviously this idea, that has so strong a hold in current morality, betrays some forgotten origin that once accounted for it rationally, but which now lies latent and unavowed among the dearest of our prejudices.

We have seen how the nebulous outlines of our social faiths were hardened, in Germany, during the time of the Reformation and the development of the great cities. During the same period, the England that her sons called "merry" was also on her deathbed, and modern England was born amidst the storm of that momentous epoch—a shadowed and care-worn land, full of toil and gloom and sorrow. One wonders for how long that strange, driven look has rested on the faces of her people, as they hurry through her brimming cities, eternally pursuing the means of existence, forgetful of its ends. True children of the Reformation, these grey and grim and business-driven hordes of men and women, enduring, in dull patience, the weariness of their lives, rigid in the observance of custom, but tolerant of the miseries that rage within and without the citadel of their conventions.

And now, looking back over the rough track that we have traversed, in the effort to obtain a general view of social history, it is easy to pick out the prominent features and to realise in what manner our present England has grown up. The result of such a bird's-eye view is not cheering. The factors are (roughly) as follows :—strict marriage, prostitution, the cultus of external sanctions, irrespective of spiritual facts ; commercialism and competition in the most exaggerated forms, the subjection of women, with their consequent purchase by men, under differing names and conditions throughout society; and finally, the (also consequent) dual moral standard for the two sexes.

We need no ghost come from the grave to tell us that from elements such as these it is morally impossible to produce a healthy society.

PART III

" There was no shame on earth too black to blacken
That much-praised woman's face."
—CHARLOTTE STETSON.

PERHAPS it may be said without much exaggeration, that
the cure for social ills is the clear realisation of their
existence. But the prescription seems simpler than it
really is. People are indeed ready enough to cry out
against the innumerable progeny of evils that spring out
of some great fundamental wrong ; but it sometimes
takes centuries before a whole nation comes to recognise
that parent-wrong, in its relationship with its vast and
objectionable family. The individuals of that family
differ among themselves, and differ according to the conditions of their age, so that in (say) the fifteenth century,
they will be fathered on one institution, and in the sixteenth, mankind will find some other contemporary abuse
on which to lay the blame of their birth. Meanwhile,
the guilty ancestor of them all lies cherished in the very
heart of the society that it ruins. We have seen that
among these patriarchs of evil, the subjection of women
must be classed. As in the case of a sufferer from
blood-poisoning, some of the symptoms may be mitigated,
but new distresses will follow the supposed cures, until
the poison itself is driven out of the system.

It has often been objected : " Granting that these
evils are born of that particular parent, how can they
be cured ? " And the answer simply is : They can be
cured only by making mankind *en masse* recognise that
they *are* the offspring of that parent. The rest follows
inevitably, if sometimes rather slowly.

92

It is with the view of tracing the career of this parent evil (viz., the relation of man to woman)- that these essays have been written. To reveal the ferocious creature, in his true colours, is to deprive him of claws and fangs and all the paraphernalia of destruction ; but the overwhelming difficulty lies in the revealing.

It is now proposed—with exactly the same object in view—to take instances from history illustrating the condition of women ; and by reminding ourselves of these well-known facts, to show how unmistakable is the ancestry of these conditions whose horror is realised in succeeding centuries, but never to the same extent in their own.

It is the habit of most people to read the chronicles of the Past as if some mystic barrier separated that by-gone period from our own enlightened times. To read thus is to lose one of the most valuable lessons of history.

The following instances are taken from Gibbon, whose impartiality on this subject cannot be questioned.

After the defeat of the Goths by the Emperor Claudius (who, nevertheless, was very anxious to improve the discipline of his troops), the Gothic women were divided into groups and allotted to the Roman soldiers—two or three to each. This proceeding was thus officially recognised, nay, ordered in one of the best-disciplined of the imperial armies, and from this much may be inferred. If the true internal history of warfare could be written, it would surely be found that the full horror of this scourge of mankind had fallen upon women.

A chief of the Roxolani had deserted the standard of Hermanric, King of the Goths, into whose power the luckless wife of the traitor chief afterwards fell. In order to revenge himself upon her husband, Hermanric ordered her to be torn asunder by wild horses. To ill-treat the property of his enemy, let it be observed, was to gratify his thirst for vengeance.

During the Gothic invasion of Greece, under Alaric,

"the beautiful women were driven away with the spoil and cattle of the flaming villages." "The female captives," Gibbon adds, "submitted to the laws of war . . . beauty was the reward of valour, and the Greeks could not reasonably complain of the abuse which was justified by the example of heroic times."

The next instance carries us to the fifth century, and to the scene of the mighty conflict between the Franks and Huns in Central Europe. The Thuringians, who served in the army of the Huns under Attila,

"massacred their hostages as well as their captives ; 200 young maidens were tortured with exquisite and unrelenting rage ; their bodies were torn asunder by wild horses ; or their bones crushed under the weight of rolling waggons ; and their unburied limbs were abandoned on the public roads, as a prey to dogs and vultures."

Without sharing in any of the excitement, the glory, or the rewards of war, women have always had to accept its worst risks, and to endure its most terrible insults.

In times of peace, men were able to defend their possessions, wives included. To dispute a monopoly in the latter kind of property has always been, and still is, the unpardonable offence. But as soon as the country was disturbed by war, houses and cities were plundered, and woman shared the fate of the rest of man's possessions.

In the "Institutes of Manu" we find precisely the same view set forth with authority ; though here, there are some faint traces of the mother-age ; as in the asserted "venerableness" of a mother, who surpasses in that quality "a thousand fathers." However, her extreme venerableness appears to avail the Indian woman but little.

"But they term the Daiva rite, the gift of a daughter, after having adorned her, to a sacrificial priest, rightly doing his work. . . ." "That is" (adds the translator in a note), "the priest who performs a sacrifice receives a maiden as part of the fee."[1]

---

[1] "Institutes of Manu." Translated by Dr Burnell.

The author of the " Institutes " makes the following assertions :—

" Houses which women, not honoured, curse ; those, as if blighted, perish utterly. . . ." Also : " Where women grieve, that family quickly perishes."

Here, again, is a faint glimpse of the ancient faith. Yet the real trend of the teaching of Manu, in common with the teaching of all prophets until this day, has been of a kind to cause women to grieve and to curse most bitterly. Perhaps that is why so many " houses " and nations have indeed utterly perished.

" Though of bad conduct and debauched " (Manu continues in his more patriarchal vein), "or even devoid of good qualities, a husband must always be worshipped like a god by a good wife."

Most English readers indignantly exclaim against this maxim ; nevertheless this is precisely the doctrine that English wives have been taught from time immemorial, though in language which veils the admonition in a manner necessary for the protection of modern sensibilities. We like to have our survivals of barbarous old doctrine expressed with true refinement. Submissive deference to the husband, simply because he *is* the husband, by the wife, simply because she *is* the wife, still remains a defended canon of feminine morality. " Of course, my dear, if your husband approves——" is a familiar phrase on the lips of women of the last generation, nor is it by any means obsolete to-day. Doubtless there is an instinctive desire on the part of many women, who were brought up in the old faith, to prevent their sisters from moving beyond the lines that bounded female existence in the earlier half of the century. The idea is entirely modern that the wife has a right to choose her own mode of existence, without waiting for her husband's permission. An amiable couple would be likely to consult one another's wishes, within reason, but the idea of " approval," in the old interpretation, belongs unmistakably to the order of sentiment which Manu set forth for the guidance of the women of India; a sentiment which there led to child-marriage, suttee, and the ill-treatment of widows.

"For women," says Manu, "there is no separate sacrifice, nor vow, nor even feast. If a woman obeys her husband, for that she is exalted to heaven."

Translate this into current terms, and we have a most familiar homily: "The true woman has no interests separate from those of her home" [no "separate vow nor feast" for *her !*] "Her highest ambitions and her noblest vocation are to be found in that sacred circle——" and so on, *ad libitum.* As for the last quoted sentence of Manu: ("If a woman obeys her husband, for that she is exalted to heaven"), Annie S. Swan gives a ready-made modern version.

"And I further hold," she says, "that having under-taken the duties and responsibilities matrimony involves, God will require at her hands an account of that steward-ship before any other." (The claims of the stewardship seem to be too manifold to leave much time for the con-struction of sentences; the one just quoted recalling the following example of similar formation: "Replying in the affirmative, the coffin-lid was again closed").

Volumes might, of course, be filled with facts gleaned from all times, illustrating the same underlying idea in its different manifestations, mild or terrible, according to the general state of civilisation of the country and the age.

There are, indeed, but few homes in England at this moment, that do not offer examples of the kind; though in many—probably in most cases—the idea on which they rest has found its least degrading and least obvious form of manifestation. Yet it is a fact, and a somewhat startling one, that the tacit beliefs on which the best of English homes are founded (setting aside, of course, unorthodox exceptions), are those which render possible and law-protected, the outrages suffered by women in the very worst.

In Mongolia, there are large cages in the market-place, wherein condemned prisoners are kept and starved to death. The people collect in front of these cages to taunt and insult the victims as they die slowly, day by day, before their eyes. In reading the history of the past, and the literature of our own day, it is difficult to avoid seeing, in that Mongolian market-place, a symbol of our own society, with its iron cage, wherein women are held in bondage, suffering moral starvation, while the thoughtless gather round to taunt their lingering misery. Let any one who thinks this exaggerated, note the manner in which our own novelists, for instance, past and present, treat all subjects connected with women, marriage and motherhood, and then let him ask himself if he does not recognise at once its ludicrous inconsistency, and its insults to womanhood, open and implied. The very respect, so-called, of man for woman, being granted solely on condition of her observing certain laws dictated by him, conceals a subtle kind of insolence. It is really the pleased approval of a lawgiver at the sight of obedient subjects.

Woman has certainly been the Ugly Duckling of society ; hunted, insulted, threatened or cajoled by her masters; scouted, scolded, admonished, betrayed; suffering all the evils of her age and country, while enjoying not a tithe of its compensating privileges ; held in tutelage, yet punished for all sins and errors with a ferocity and a persistence specially reserved for the sex which is called weak ; and specially directed against those who are held incapable of the responsibilities of freedom and of citizenship. Truly the fate of woman, in its injustice, its debasement and humiliating pain, is a tragedy such as Shakespeare never wrote nor Æschylus dreamt of.

PART IV

" So each new man strikes root into a far-fore time."—MATTHEW ARNOLD.

UP to the present day, the sentiments naturally attendant on the purchase system of marriage have received no serious check.

In strict accordance with hereditary preconceptions, civilised women have been carefully trained, while the ideas of young men are developed on lines that accurately correspond, so that the type of conduct and sentiments to which the young girl is educated, is exactly that which the young man has learnt to expect; or if it is not always *quite* so exact as he might wish, the difference is scornfully set down to the discredit of the rebel; and when such differences become too numerous, loud lamentations arise, and prophecies become frequent of the approaching collapse of society.

However, on the whole, the young man has had little reason to complain. Departures from the antique pattern of feminine excellence have been rare indeed, considering the rigidity of that pattern, and the tremendous forces which it at once concealed and rendered futile. The model has been accepted with scarcely a murmur, and followed, perforce, for centuries with such fidelity that no other design has seemed even possible to most of us, much less preferable.

To the preservation of orthodoxy on these subjects, our conditions have of course brought powerful assistance. While marriage remained practically the only means of livelihood for women, there was little danger of their seeing too clearly the seamy side of the arrangement; for to see *that* would be to stand helpless and open-eyed between the alternatives of selling themselves for a livelihood, and starvation; or, in milder cases, between the alternatives of social failure, and a marriage which, without being altogether worldly, would yet never for a moment, have been thought of in the entire absence of the worldly motive.

If the position was to remain tolerable at all, obviously it must not be looked in the face. Therefore the pretence must be cherished that the mere form of marriage makes the purchased condition an honourable one. Thousands of respectable women feel in their heart of hearts its real nature, but for that very reason, they try to buttress their self-respect by angry denial.[1]

Kirke White's *Ode to Thought* is singularly expressive of their condition of mind. Thought, indeed for women, has ever been a vindictive companion!

> " Hence, away, vindictive Thought!
> Thy pictures are of pain ;
> The visions through thy dark eye caught,
> They with no gentle charms are fraught,
> So prithee back again.
> I would not weep,
> I wish to sleep,
> Then why, thou busy foe, with me thy vigils keep ? "

Of what avail, then, is it to inveigh against mercenary marriages, however degrading they may be, when a glance at the position of affairs shows that there is, for the average woman, no reasonable alternative? We cannot expect, even if we ask, every woman to be a dauntless heroine, and to choose a hard and thorny path when a comparatively smooth one (as it seems) offers itself, and, moreover, when the pressure of public opinion urges strongly in that direction. A few braver natures will resist, to swell the crowd of worn-out, underpaid

[1] See "Married Life, Present and Future," note 1, p. 139.

workers, but the majority will take the voice of Society for the voice of God, or, at any rate, of wisdom, and our common respectable marriage—upon which the safety of all social existence is supposed to rest—will remain, as it is now, the worst, because the most hypocritical form of woman-purchase.

Few people, when brought face to face with the problem, can be found to approve of mercenary unions. They blame, however, not the social order, but the *victims* of that order : the unfortunate girls whose horizon is as limited as their opportunities, whose views of life are cribbed, cabined, and confined by their surroundings, whose very right and wrong, just and unjust, are chosen for them. They act as they are taught to act, behaving precisely as every average person behaves—viz., in exact obedience to the public opinion of his little world.

"Yes, marriage is often a failure," say the orthodox reproachfully ; " it is entered into too early, too thoughtlessly, without (on the part of the wife) a knowledge of cooking and the domestic arts, without a flawless temper, without absolute immunity from headaches. Society and the institution of marriage are not to blame, only the faulty individuals who marry."

Alas, for much instructed, much badgered, much belaboured individuals ! Like the absent, they are always in the wrong ! The last person who could be justly blamed for the marriage failure is the girl who acts according to universal example and precept.

It is impossible for an outsider to realise the restrictions and narrowness of the average girl's life. We are too near to the result to be able to see it. When some one points out that the education has been distorting, we, on our side, point beamingly to some of its disastrous consequences, and say, " Behold, the Eternal has so willed it. Thus was the young person designed by Nature from the beginning."

And this is the bewildered being, stunted in intelligence, in self-respect; with a swollen, unwholesome conscience, spreading in all directions like some rankly-growing gourd, increasing not in harmony with, but at the expense of the other sides of the nature—this is the ill-treated being who is held responsible for the failure of marriage, the victim to whom a logical society says : "Marry, and ask no questions ; who are you that you should criticise an institution which has lasted for centuries ? Marriage is your natural career, your own highly-developed conscience must tell you so. If you do not adopt it, well, we fear you will find cause to regret your decision. If you can't secure a husband, we can but regard you as a failure, a supernumerary who has no proper place in the world." So the bewildered being turns an alarmed ear to the counsel that greets her on every side, in one form or another, open or disguised ; for it is not only from the lips of worldlings that these warnings issue. People know better than to appeal merely to the self-interest of a being possessing such a magnificent overgrowth of conscience. The being can be led ; she need not be driven. Society appeals to her gourd and wins an easy victory. But alas, for the poor Young Person ! With all her dutiful submission, her marriage is not happy. There is no real community of thought between the pair. The wife means well—what else has she a gourd for ?— but of what avail is this, if the best that she can do is to obey her husband ? There are few men who do not deserve something more, and none who would not tend to deteriorate under such temptations to egotism. The wife meanwhile suffers, as she feels her husband drifting from her, but she says nothing. He is the last person to guess how lonely and how sad her life is. "Until a woman cries, men never think she is suffering ; bless their block-headism ! " exclaims Mrs Carlyle.

And all this springs, not in the main from the faults of the individual, but from the fault of the tradition, which thus inspires the wife, when most desirous of doing her duty, to suppress all that is individual in herself, while it encourages the husband to expect such deference as his right.[1] This idea that the wife should subordinate her dominant interests is perhaps one of the most frequent causes of colourless and monotonous homes. "There's no place like home—and a good thing, too!" some contributor to *Punch* recklessly exclaims. Out of such homes springs a second crop of bewildered beings, whose only sin is obedience, but upon whose shoulders is piled almost all the blame of our unsuccessful marriages. Not only the absent but the sinned-against are always in the wrong. To encourage a child to put a lighted match to a train of gunpowder and then to punish him because he has caused a disastrous explosion is neither wise nor just.

On the other hand, if a woman remains single, her lot, under present social conditions, is often a very sad one. Bebel is eloquent upon the sufferings of unmarried women, which must be keen indeed for those who have been prepared for marriage and for nothing else, whose emotions have been coloured solely by pictures of domestic happiness. To the eye that is trained in so one-sided a fashion as to be able to see the colour red and no other, grey indeed will the universe appear if all red objects be withdrawn from it.

Mrs Augusta Webster amusingly points out the inconsistencies of popular notions on this subject. She says :—

[1] " Instead of boiling up individuals into the species, I would draw a chalk line round each individuality and preach to it to keep within that and to preserve and cultivate its identity at the expense of ever so much lost gilt of other people's 'isms '."—Mrs Carlyle.

"People think women who do not want to marry unfeminine; people think women who *do* want to marry immodest: people combine both opinions by regarding it as unfeminine for women not to look forward longingly to wifehood as the hope and purpose of their lives, and ridiculing and contemning any individual woman of their acquaintance whom they suspect of entertaining such a longing. They must wish and not wish; they must by no means give and they must certainly not withhold encouragement—and so it goes on, each precept cancelling the last, and most of them negative."

There are, doubtless, equally absurd prejudices which hamper a man's freedom by teaching girls and their friends to look for proposals of marriage, instead of regarding signs of interest in a more wholesome spirit. It is certain that we shall never have a world really worth living in, until men and women can show interest in one another without being driven either to marry, or to forego altogether the pleasure and the profit of frequent meeting. Nor will the world be really a pleasant world while it continues to make friendship between persons of opposite sexes wellnigh impossible, by insisting that they *are* so, and thereby, in a thousand direct and indirect ways, bringing about the fulfilment of its own prophecy. All this false sentiment, with the restrictions it implies, makes the ideal marriage—that is, a union prompted by harmony of nature and by friendship—almost beyond the reach of this generation.

It may be worth while to quote here a typical example of some letters written to Max O'Rell, on the publication of *The Daughters of John Bull*. One lady of direct language exclaims fiercely, "Man is a beast!", and she goes on to explain in gleeful strains that, having been left a small fortune by a relative, she is able to dispense with the society of "the odious creature." (Of course Max O'Rell warmly congratulates the "odious creature.")

"At last," another lady bursts forth, "we have some one among us with wit to perceive that the life which a woman leads with the ordinary sherry-drinking, cigar-smoking husband is no better than that of an Eastern slave. Take my own case, which is that of thousands of others in our land. I belong to my lord and master, body and soul. The duties of a housekeeper, upper nurse, and governess are required of me. I am expected to be always at home, at my husband's beck and call. It is true that he feeds me, and that for his own glorification he gives me handsome clothing. It is also true that he does not beat me. For this I ought, of course, to be duly grateful ; but I often think of what you say on the wife and servant question, and wonder how many of us would like to have the cook's privilege of being able to give warning to leave."

If the wife feels thus, we may be sure the husband thinks he has his grievances also ; and when we place this description side by side with that of the unhappy plight of bored husbands commiserated by Mrs Lynn Linton, there is no escaping the impression that there is something very "rotten in the state of Denmark." Amongst other absurdities, we have well-meaning husbands and wives harassing one another to death, for no reason in the world but the desire of conforming to current notions regarding the proper conduct of married people. These victims are expected to go about perpetually together, as if they were a pair of carriage-horses ; to be for ever holding claims over one another, exacting or making useless sacrifices, and generally getting in one another's way, with a diligence and self-forgetfulness that would be admirable were it not so supremely ridiculous. The man who marries finds that his liberty has gone, and the woman exchanges one set of restrictions for another. She thinks herself neglected if the husband does not always return to her in the evenings, and the husband and society think her undutiful, frivolous, and so forth, if she does not stay at home alone, trying to sigh him back again. The luckless man finds his wife so *very* much confined to her "proper sphere," that she is, perchance, more exemplary than entertaining. Still, she may look injured and resigned, but she must not seek society and occupation on her own account, bringing new interest and knowledge into the joint existence, and becoming thus a contented, cultivated, and agreeable human being. No wonder that, while all this is forbidden, we have so many unhappy wives and bored husbands. The more admirable the wives, the more profoundly bored the husbands.

Doubtless there are bright exceptions to this picture of married life, but we are not dealing with exceptions. In most cases, the chain of marriage frets and chafes, if it does not make a serious wound; and where there is happiness—as we are so often assured that there is—it is dearly bought, and is not often on a very high plane. For husband and wife are then apt to forget everything in the narrow interests of their home, to depend entirely upon one another, to steep themselves in the same ideas, till they become mere echoes, half-creatures, useless to their kind, because they have let individuality die. There are few things more stolidly irritating than a very "united" couple. The likeness in appearance and gesture that may often be remarked between married people, is a melancholy instance of this communal form of degeneration. This condition, be it observed, is the very antithesis of that deep and real unity of two individualities, which are harmonious just because they are *not* identical—as two colours, for example, may be exquisite in harmony, where a mere repetition of the same tint, in two nominally separate objects, would create nothing but a tiring monotony.

The tyrannical spirit has little or no check under present conditions of married life, for the despot—male or female—knows that the victim must bear whatever has to be borne without hope of relief on this side the grave; except when the grievance is of such a nature as to come within the reach of the law; a wide enough margin to give scope to sufficiently serious cases of tyranny, as probably nobody would attempt to deny.

This tyranny takes various forms; many of them—and these are perhaps the most difficult to deal with—

G

being based upon pleas of love and devotion; a devotion
which claimants have no weak idea of presenting gratis.
Often the tyranny expresses itself profitably by appeals
to the pity and the conscience of the victims; by
threats of the suffering that will ensue to the despot, if
his wishes are heartlessly disregarded.   Should these
measures fail, more drastic methods are adopted.   There
are stern or pathetic reminders of indisputable claims,
accusations of selfishness, of failing duty, and so forth.
Between married people, this system is carried to its
extreme, and derives much of its power from the support of popular sentiment.

Upon the legal bond is founded every sort of senti-
mental tie, till at last the couple so bind and entwine
themselves with multitudinous restrictions, that every
vestige of freedom disappears, and obligation enters
into the very citadel of the heart.   All spontaneity
must and does evidently depart, and if feelings so bullied
and pinioned show the tendency of all prisoners to
escape, then loud are the wailings of the injured one,
who has succeeded at last in worrying affection to
death.   The luxury of a grievance is the sole remaining
consolation.   It seems strange that, with so long an
experience behind them, human beings have not yet
learnt that, though they may obtain dominion by
making large demands, they are likely to win regard
in inverse proportion to their claims; and that, in any
case, it is a little absurd to set up an injured and fretful
demand for affection, as if it could be laid on with the gas
and the water, and kept going in regular quarterly supplies.
Even when such conduct does not destroy attachment,
it does what perhaps is worse; it destroys individuality.

There must be a perpetual surrender of tastes and
opportunities, in deference to the affectionate selfishness
of the devoted partner, who is unable to realise that
what may seem trivial to him is a matter of importance
to some one else.   The husband cannot bear to be

that, without this coercion on the part of the State, we
should have irresponsible coercion on the part of individuals. The problem of the children is generally urged
as the plea for forcing parents to remain together against
their will. But the excuse cannot be considered good
enough even at the moment, and every advance made
by humanity in developing its sympathies, steadily
weakens the force of the plea.

The injustice of obliging two people, on pain of social
ostracism, either to accept the marriage-contract as it
stands, or to live apart, is surely self-evident. If the
contract were to be made more glaringly absurd, every
one would recognise the wrong. For instance—as the
Pall Mall Gazette once pointed out—if it were to be
decreed that the woman, in order to be legally married,
must gouge out her right eye, no sane person would
argue that the marriage-contract was perfectly just,
simply because the woman was at liberty to remain
single if she did not relish the conditions. Yet this
argument is used on behalf of the present contract, as if
it were really any sounder in the one case than in the
other. The existing conditions, being less obviously
terrible, are put up with, but they remain unfair notwithstanding. Nobody is actually forced by police
regulation to buy adulterated food ; no man is forced to
take a farm under conditions which he thinks unjust ;
yet we do not on that account consider food adulteration
permissible, or rack-renting blameless.

Certain aspects of the contract question are well
brought out in a book which has been quoted against
me.[1]

"'If I signed a contract,' Ideala explained, 'and found out afterwards that those who induced me to become a party to it had kept
me in ignorance of the most important clause in it, could you call
that a moral contract ?'

---

[1] "Ideala." A Study from Life.

mined mathematically by the extent and the character of individual consciousness. All that tends to narrow and stunt this, narrows and stunts the life of the whole race, and retards its growth. Popular sentiment is busy at this stunting process. Thus we find the system almost reducing itself to absurdity in orthodox family life, wherein—speaking roughly—all approved persons are conducting their existence, not according to their own convictions, but according to those of some affectionate relative. In short, every estimable person is acting vicariously on the motives of somebody else.

We come to the conclusion, that the present form of marriage—exactly in proportion to its conformity with orthodox ideas—is a failure. If certain unconscious heretics, ignoring the teachings of orthodoxy, have given us inspiring examples of what marriage might be and can be, such instances afford no argument in favour of the institution as it is at present interpreted. Just to the extent to which a union follows that popular interpretation, is it a degrading bondage.

These are hard words, yet many more years will not pass away before most thinking people admit them to be justified.

*   *   *   *   *   *

The coercive element in marriage, be it observed, has been introduced as a crude corrective to the utter helplessness to which law-aided custom has reduced women. Wives (as it is even now argued) would be deserted by their husbands and left to starve, unless the law compelled the latter to remain with them. To place women in such a position that they need no longer chain unwilling husbands to their side from sheer dread of starvation, does not appear a particularly shocking proposition, when looked at calmly. When we are assured that marriage is really for the protection of the woman, there is indeed some truth in the assertion. She has been brought to a position which obliges the law to come to her aid, now and then. Her capital (as so many men have naïvely pointed out, without the faintest suspicion of the terrible wrong implied by the fact) consists in her youth, beauty, and attractions. She must invest it in marriage, and Society offers a guarantee for the payment of the interest. Such is the protection that marriage offers to women !

There are many signs that this arrangement is ceasing to be satisfying to either sex. They both more or less chafe against the commercial element, which social conditions still prevent them from either abolishing or ignoring. An increasing number of women are refusing a life of comparative ease in marriage, rather than enter upon it as a means of livelihood, for which their freedom has to be sacrificed. As this sentiment grows general, men and women cannot fail to recognise, as a mere truism, that so long as affection and friendship remain between a married couple, no bonds are necessary to hold them united ; but that when these cease, the tie becomes intolerable, and no law ought to have power to enforce it. It need scarcely be added that there are, in these days, a growing number who insist that there must be complete acknowledgment of the right of the woman to possess herself, body and soul, in absolute independence. It has been part and parcel of her slave's position that this right has hitherto been denied her, by the sentiment of her contemporaries, nay, until the decision in the Jackson case, by force of law.

As the monogamic ideal becomes more and more realised and followed, not from force but from conviction, increasing freedom in the form of marriage must—paradox as it sounds—be looked for among a developing people. Greater respect for the liberties of the individual would alone dictate a system less barbaric, and would secure it from danger of abuse.

It must not be forgotten that all these anticipated changes cannot but be dependent on the educating influences that are brought to bear on the younger genera-

tion. Instead of separating girls and boys during their
early years, we shall learn to educate them together,
and thus lay the foundation, from the very beginning, of
a wholesome community of interests, without which no
marriage can be otherwise than disappointing.

It is our present absurd interference with the civilising influences of one sex upon the other, that initiates
and enhances many of the dangers and difficulties of our
social life, and gives colour to popular fears.

Anyone who imagines that he can destroy a social
fact by attacking its figure-head, is hopeful rather
than wise. It is not marriage *per se*, but the whole
social drift with which it is at present co-related, that
constitutes the evil. We must look not for destruction,
but for re-birth. The essential wrongs on which I have
been insisting—being wrongs of thought and sentiment
—are destined to give way before a vigorous moral
Renaissance, which has already begun. Few close
observers can have failed to recognise, amidst the remarkable tumult of thought during the last few years,
signs and wonders which seem to herald an awakening
of this nature. These new ideas—like waves on an
iron-bound coast—create not a little clamour as they
beat upon the granite of age-long creed and custom.
That clamour attests their reality and their strength.

That this change should be hotly opposed for a season
is not a matter for regret. Ideas on which the fate of
humanity may depend, could not be safely admitted without at least some preliminary processes of threshing, by
which one may hope the chaff may be separated from
the grain. The majority still believe, and must continue to believe for a long time to come, that there is
nothing but danger in any doctrine which disturbs, by
one hairsbreadth, the present conceptions of the conjugal
relations. That majority will continue their work on
the threshing-floor, perhaps helping rather than hinder-
ing that which they desire to oppose. The new ideal

must submit to the process for the appointed years of its probation.

The changes suggested here, involve an immense increase of complexity, a widening of the human horizon. We are, in fact, contemplating a stupendous step of racial progress. There is a whole world yet to explore in the direction of social developments, and it is more than probable that the future holds a discovery in the domain of spirit as great as that of Columbus in the domain of matter.

THE FUTURE OF THE HOME

THE FUTURE OF THE HOME

" Eccentricity has always abounded when strength of character has abounded. That so few now dare to be eccentric marks the chief danger of the time."—
J. S. MILL.

THE practical man believes in what may be called the pendulum theory of history ; he sees in social movements a mere *oscillation,* a motion to and fro, without any real progress. As for the misery and vice in which the vast majority of mankind are plunged, that is eternal and inevitable.

The Meliorist believes, on the contrary, that there is a cure for these things, slow but certain, and that it lies, like a concealed treasure, in the sympathetic and rational impulses of man's nature, which may be developed to so triumphant a dominion that they will finally subdue the savage and sensual instincts, even if they do not alto-gether destroy them. " Education is the sum of habits."[1] This, then, is the theory upon which reader and writer must agree, for the sake of argument. It is, in fact, the theory of evolution.

Evolution ! the word awes us. We are like children frightened at our own shadows ; like the shepherd on the Brocken, who mistakes his own exaggerated image on the clouds that sweep over the mountain-summit, for some angry spirit of the storm. There will come a time—it is close upon us—when the cloud image will cease to mean for us a spirit more powerful than our-selves. We raise our arm, the shadow-form raises his arm also : he is our slave, we can command his every movement.

[1] " Heredity."—Ribot.

Belief in the power of man to choose his direction of change :—this is the creed of the future, and it will soon come to be the distinctive mark of the essentially modern thinker.

Given this belief, that man is arbiter of his own destiny, it becomes obviously right to strive to realise even the most difficult of our ideals, knowing that if only it be in the true line of progress, the struggle towards it will bring us to higher ground, even should we fail to achieve what we are striving after, exactly in the form we desired.

We ought to sanction no compromise except for the sake of the ideal itself. For instance, freedom of marriage being our aim, we must yet endure some compromise, as best we may, though only for the sake of that very aim, because we know, or believe, that an attempt at complete emancipation would, in fact, create complete thraldom, for licence is in its nature despotic. In our zeal for the cause of freedom, it is only too easy to sin against her. But every restraint which is placed upon the actions of men ought to be placed upon them in the name of liberty, and never by one hairsbreadth beyond what is needed for the purpose of avoiding the agressions of those who do not understand what liberty means. The true lover of freedom loves it for others as well as for himself.

> " If ye do not feel the chain
> When it works a brother's pain,
> Are ye not base slaves indeed ?
> Slaves unworthy to be freed ? "

Now, our present marriage system is coercive. The marriage contract is the only contract which we have to submit to without having a voice in the framing of its conditions ; the only contract, moreover, which lasts for life. It is entirely arbitrary, and nothing could justify it except the certainty (which does not exist) that, without this coercion on the part of the State, we should have irresponsible coercion on the part of individuals. The problem of the children is generally urged as the plea for forcing parents to remain together against their will. But the excuse cannot be considered good enough even at the moment, and every advance made by humanity in developing its sympathies, steadily weakens the force of the plea.

The injustice of obliging two people, on pain of social ostracism, either to accept the marriage-contract as it stands, or to live apart, is surely self-evident. If the contract were to be made more glaringly absurd, every one would recognise the wrong. For instance—as the *Pall Mall Gazette* once pointed out—if it were to be decreed that the woman, in order to be legally married, must gouge out her right eye, no sane person would argue that the marriage-contract was perfectly just, simply because the woman was at liberty to remain single if she did not relish the conditions. Yet this argument is used on behalf of the present contract, as if it were really any sounder in the one case than in the other. The existing conditions, being less obviously terrible, are put up with, but they remain unfair notwithstanding. Nobody is actually forced by police regulation to buy adulterated food; no man is forced to take a farm under conditions which he thinks unjust; yet we do not on that account consider food adulteration permissible, or rack-renting blameless.

Certain aspects of the contract question are well brought out in a book which has been quoted against me.[1]

"'If I signed a contract,' Ideala explained, 'and found out afterwards that those who induced me to become a party to it had kept me in ignorance of the most important clause in it, could you call that a moral contract?'

---

[1] "Ideala." A Study from Life.

" 'I should say that people had not dealt fairly with you,' the Bishop avowed ; 'but there might be nothing in the clause to which you could object.'

" 'But suppose there was something in the clause to which I very strongly objected, that was repugnant to my whole moral nature ; and suppose I was forced by the law to fulfil it nevertheless, should you not say that in acting against my conscience I acted immorally ?'

" We all fell into the trap, and looked an encouraging assent.

" 'And in that case,' she continued, 'I suppose my duty would be to evade the law, and act on my own conscience. I should be only doing what the early martyrs had to do.'

" 'But I don't see what particular contract you are thinking of,' said the lawyer.

" 'The marriage-contract,' Ideala answered calmly."

Ideala further alarms the Law and the Church by insisting that " only the love that lasts can sanctify marriage, and a marriage without such love is an immoral contract."

The Bishop becomes piteous, and promises to preach a sermon next Sunday on the subject. If he succeeded in showing that Ideala was wrong in her opinion, he must have been a shining light and a pillar of the Church indeed !

Now, some of the most mischievous elements of our present family life are created by the submissive attitude of the woman. It is impossible to describe, much more to overstate the far-reaching evil which it fosters. Disobedience, in the present crisis of affairs, is woman's first duty. " That will lose her her power," some one exclaims, " the power that she now possesses ; the sceptre which, if cleverly wielded, might move the world." That power, however, is but a power that is won by smiles and wiles and womanly devices ; and, when won, is hers, not by right, but by favour. This is the power, not of a free being, but of a favourite slave. When shall we come to see that such a conception of woman's influence is mean, ignoble, *ugly*, through and through ? When shall we banish these remnants of Eastern despotism from our homes, these haunting whispers from lands which we profess to despise ? We are outgrowing these conceptions; but oh, how slowly ! Hamerton, the author of the *Intellectual Life*, is one of the few men who have entirely outgrown them.

" If the reader," he says, "has ever had a travelling companion, some person totally unsuited to his nature, and quite unable to enter into the ideas that chiefly interest him ; unable to see even the things that he sees, and always ready to treat negligently or contemptuously the thoughts and preferences that are most his own ; he will have some faint conception of what it must be to find oneself tied to an unsuitable companion for the tedious journey of this mortal life ; and if, on the other hand, he has ever enjoyed the pleasure of wandering through a country that interested him, along with a friend who could understand his interest and share it, and whose society enhanced the charm of every prospect and banished dulness from the dreariest inns, he may, in some poor and imperfect degree, realise the happiness of those who have chosen the life-companion wisely."

How can a wife, trained to mere submission and " duty," ever hope to enjoy a companionship of this last inspiring kind, and what man worth his salt would really prefer to it the joy of undisputed mastership ?

The following quotation points to the fact or theory that while we are burdened with our present ideas about matrimony, it is necessarily more or less unhappy if one of the pair happens to possess an original bent of mind, still more so if that originality is accompanied by exceptional talent.

" High intellect is in itself a peculiarity, in a certain sense it is really an eccentricity, even when so thoroughly sane and rational as in the case of George Eliot and Mill. It is an eccentricity in this sense, that its mental centre does not coincide with that of ordinary people—if there is the touch of original talent or genius in one of the parties, it is sure to result in many ideas that will lie outside of any local common-sense, and then the other party, living in that sense, will consider those ideas peculiar and perhaps deplorable. Here then are elements of dissension lying quite ready, like explosive materials—the merest accident may shatter in a moment the whole fabric of affection."

We ought all to be taught, at the same time as we learn to say "please" and "thank you," and not to make a grab, during meals, at some tit-bit upon which we have set our hearts, that to respect the freedom of others—not even excepting our relations or our life-companion—is one of the first duties of civilised life, the neglect of which is sheer aggression. Hamerton points out, that in order to keep the peace and imitate successful marriage, "the more enlightened and intelligent of the two parties has to stifle half his nature."

And this is the admirable institution which watches over the interests of society, and strangles discreetly those of her members who are able to instil fresh life into her, and to keep her pure and sane and sound! The policy resembles that of a gardener, who should snap off the leading shoots of his young pine trees!

This tendency, in fact, constitutes the great danger of the age. We deify the Average. Unless a rebellion against this idol shortly takes place, we shall sink into a condition of *bourgeois* Philistinism which makes one's hair stand on end to contemplate. If a desperate person under that *régime*, committed bigamy or trigamy, or any other crime, for a diversion, he would certainly do it under what a friend of Mrs Carlyle calls "attenuating circumstances."

Mrs Grundy in black silk, with a sceptre in her hand, on the throne of the Ages, supported by an angel-choir of Young Persons! Is this to be the end of our democracy? There are ominous signs of it. One is forced regretfully to acknowledge the fidelity to nature of the description in the Nonsense Songs and Stories of the visiting acquaintance of the seven unfortunate families, which, we are told, "was very numerous, and distinguished, and select, and responsible, and ridiculous." [1]

[1] Edward Lear.

The dominant type in well-to-do communities is growing ever more "numerous and responsible and ridiculous," and variations from that type less frequent. Poetry survives in the heavy atmosphere only with an effort: romance languishes: painting and sculpture are distinguished by "a serene and sickly suavity only known to the truly virtuous."

This constitutes a very serious danger. We must consent to give play to the individual, or our democratic institutions will plunge us into a slavery from which there is no redemption. In many of our imagined safeguards against disorder lurks our greatest peril. We stand confronted with what a master of mixed metaphor calls "barricades in sheep's clothing."

It is in deference to our deity—"the greatest number"—that wives are exhorted to endure the miseries, even the indignities, of an unhappy marriage, rather than weaken by their rebellion the power of the legal tie.

In short, the rights of minorities are absolutely *nil*, in spite of the fiction that all citizens stand equal before the law; the sufferings of the exceptional person, whether as regards character or circumstance, being disregarded, on the ground that they happen seldom.

The infrequency of an occurrence, in any case, does not, in the slightest degree, alter the nature or bitterness of the sufferings; if an evil is intolerable, it is equally so whether one or many suffer it, and society is not just but tyrannical, when it asks its members to endure it in silence. There are miseries which no one ought to be called upon to endure by the laws of his country, which everyone is justified in resisting at all hazards, and in spite of every law, written and unwritten. Passive endurance, in such cases, is not for the good of the "greatest number"; it is simply for the degradation of human beings and the torture of human minds; and by that, the "greatest number" never reaped a benefit. Even if it did, it ought not to exact this awful sacrifice.

H

Of what value is the "good of the community," if in that community individuals can suffer thus, under the wing of the Law ? What is the meaning of the term "the welfare of society," if not the security of the individuals composing it ?

There is no virtue in mere *number.* It is an abstraction, an unreality. We have still to learn that the only things that actually exist are individual cases, and that it is John and Jemima who suffer, and not abstract masses which we call, for convenience, the greater or the less.

Marriage under reformed conditions would help to prevent the immolation of minorities, and the injury to the majority which all such sacrifices really inflict. It is impossible to wound one part of the social organism without hurting the whole, just as, happily, one cannot make one person healthier and nobler, without bestowing the same qualities, in some slight degree, upon the commonwealth of which he is a member.

> "No life
> Can be pure in its purpose and strong in its strife,
> And all life not be stronger and purer thereby."

There is yet another aspect of the question that ought not to be overlooked.

Laws are intended to restrain people from sinning against the life and welfare of others; they are not instituted for the purpose of forcing a rich crop of Christian martyrs. A man or woman may regard it as an imperative duty to accept martyrdom in marriage, in order to show reverence for the institution, or for the majesty of the law. Within limits, the State is ready to permit self-immolation, but it goes altogether beyond its sphere when it *demands* it of the average human being.

The law has no business to require martyrdom from any one. That is a matter to be settled with a man's own conscience. It is a most common and dangerous mistake to suppose that, because a course of action may be in accordance with the highest morality, the law is justified in making that action compulsory. The question for the State to decide is rather negative than positive. It ought to decree what its members may *not* do, rather than what they *must* do. A man may take upon himself a duty which would be ludicrous for the State to require of him—such, for instance, as adopting and educating the orphan children of a friend.

In the same way, a woman may regard it as a duty to endure the worst miseries of an unhappy marriage, although conscious that she has been forced or persuaded into it, when not experienced enough to judge for herself. But that is her own affair; society has no right to force upon her the martyrdom which her conscience induces her to take upon herself.

It is better to suffer certain evils than to cure them at the expense of individual freedom, because to curtail that freedom is to cut away part of the foundation of further progress. Freedom is more valuable than even a great benefit for which freedom must be sacrificed. Evils are inevitable while half-educated people are at liberty to blunder at large, yet the worst of these evils is as nothing to the burden of paternal government and illiberal institutions.

In attempting to shake off the yoke of paternal government in marriage, care must be taken to preserve the reverence for monogamy which has been slowly acquired among civilised peoples, since—among many other reasons—experience has shown this to be the only form of sex relationship which permits the progress of the race.

(It is amusing to note, in passing, that monogamy, like polygamy, has its enemies on the ground of immorality. The Mrs Grundys of the Zambesi were horribly shocked when they heard of the English custom of monogamy. The Makololo women, according to Livingstone, did not think it at all respectable; no doubt they hurried all their young persons out of earshot as rapidly as they could.)

" It is clear," says Herbert Spencer, " that monogamy has long been growing innate in the civilised man. For all the ideas and sentiments now associated with marriage have, as their inspiration, singleness of union." [1] He traces an interesting connection between polygamy and the militant type of society, and between monogamy and industrialism; he shows that war is the enemy of monogamy and of woman. War, in killing off so many young men, brings about that inconvenient disparity between the numbers of the sexes which creates many of our present difficulties. We find, then, that all modern reforms—notably those in the direction of international intercourse, brotherly co-operation and peace—tend towards the same distant goal beyond our present horizon, and that no ideal can possibly be realised by itself—a solitary space of calm in a raging sea—but only in connection, direct and indirect, with the other ideals of the age.

But however much we may have to compromise for the sake of the ideal, that ideal itself must not be compromised. There is no rational limit to the principle of liberty; moderation in liberty is as ridiculous as

---

[1] " We have strong ground for believing that permanence in marriage relations is a mark of a higher civilisation and higher types of character. But do not let us forget that the outward union must be based upon the inward union. If union be only the result of external authority, or power of external kind, it becomes a mere superstition, a fetter. There can be nothing which so lowers our view of marriage as the belief that for the imagined good of society two people whose lives and aims are inharmonious should, by a sort of external coercion, be bound together; as if society had ever been benefited by sacrificing the individual. Here, as everywhere else, freedom must be our guide. In all great matters of human feeling, not only the higher forms, but even the conception of the higher forms, can only be reached through freedom."—Auberon Herbert.

moderation in truth, or health, or happiness. Absolute liberty, then, in the relations of men and women is indeed the ideal; a limited ideal is as ludicrous as a limited belief in the axioms of geometry.

In a still distant condition of society, it is probable that unions may exist outside the law but inside society; men and women caring only for the real bond between them, and treating as of quite minor importance the artificial or legal tie.[1] So that gradually the State may come to have very little part in marriages. The tendency will be gradually to substitute internal for external law; social sentiment for anti-social license.[2]

This tendency to lay more stress on the real bond than on the artificial, can be studied, to good purpose, by comparing different countries. Wherever we find affection in marriage regarded as essential, or desirable, there we have a higher form of society, a higher level of morality, and, above all, a more progressive tendency. Beginning with pure savagery, we pass to more or less civilised countries in different stages of development— India, Persia, China, Turkey, Italy, Germany, France, America, and England (the list is not intended to be arranged in order of precedence). The rule holds good, more or less strictly, in all these cases. And now the foremost countries have to go a step further, and emphasise still more the importance of the bond of affection and friendship. In connection with this part of the subject, Mrs Carlyle's delightful comment must not be forgotten. "I do think," she says, "there is much truth in the German idea, that marriage is a

---

[1] Everything has its comic side. "On accuse Henri VIII.," says Madame de Flamareil, alluding to his treatment of his wives, "moi, je le comprends, et je l'absous; c'était un cœur généreux; lorsqu'il ne les aimait plus, il les tuait." This is carrying the doctrine of the sanction by affection almost too far!

[2] "Changes which may further facilitate divorce under certain conditions are changes which will make those conditions more and more rare." —Herbert Spencer, "Principles of Sociology," vol. i. chap. xii.

shockingly immoral institution, as well as what we have
long known it for—an extremely disagreeable one."

Marriage has been defined as a contract between two
persons and the State. Because of the children, the
State is said to have a special concern in the matter.

This is no doubt true, but it means rather less than is
generally supposed.

The State has a concern in everything that affects a
human being, down to the minutest details of his daily
life. It matters to the State every time a man smokes
more cigars than are good for him, every time a woman
pinches in her waist. It matters to the State very
much when men grow absorbed in the business of
money-making, and have no time or ability to assist in
the development of a higher type of manhood. It
matters to the State, perhaps even more, when women
give themselves up wholly to the care of their house-
holds and the rearing of their children, rendering themselves unfit for their task, and sending forth into the
already over-burdened world, swarms of ill-trained,
stupid, prejudiced human beings, to complicate still
further our complex problems. All these things concern the State nearly, but the State cannot send in-
spectors into our homes to count the cigars of the men,
and inquire into the system of education adopted by
the women. In the marriage contract, the State has a
deep concern, but it does not follow therefrom that it
has a right to interfere.

Now, if we conclude that it *has* no right to interfere,
the question arises : How can it withdraw its interference without causing social confusion ? The answer
seems plain. By a gradual widening of the limitations
within which individuals might be allowed to draw up
their private contracts, until, finally, moral standards
had risen sufficiently high to enable the State to cease
from interfering in private concerns altogether.

It is clear that legal relaxation can never take the

place of moral development; but the time seems ripe for some reform in the marriage laws. For *perfect* freedom of contract, however, freedom for woman is an essential which, of course, implies perfect legal and social equality of the sexes. And this, again, would imply an ungrudging recognition, that the work of woman in the home is not less work and not less deserving of reward and independence than when it is done amid the tumult of the industrial world.

Those two conditions, therefore, may be noted as essential to radical improvement. Indeed, we may say that they would compel it. And thus we see (in broad outline) how the great reform can be accomplished safely.

THE MORALITY OF MARRIAGE

PART I

" Before being a wife or mother, one is a human being, and neither motherly nor wifely destination can overbalance or replace the human, but must become its means, not end. As above the poet, the painter, or the hero, so above the mother does the human being rise pre-eminent."—JEAN PAUL RICHTER.

" IF it were not for the children, I would take a dose of chloroform to-morrow ! "

These are the words of the wife of a well-to-do tradesman, who, after twelve years of marriage, finds life a burden too heavy to be borne. After much theory, a little fact, hot from the lips of a simple-minded woman, without theories, but with plenty of experience, comes with a force that is somewhat startling.

The woman recognised gratefully her worldly prosperity ; there was nothing fretful about her complaints. One pitied her most when she made some unconscious admission, let fall some pathetic, patient little word, which revealed how little she asked and how much she was ready to endure. Her husband is a " good fellow," with an uncertain temper. He is capricious and imprudent, and the success of the business depends on his wife, who works at it unremittingly, sending her husband and children away for a holiday now and then, while she remains to look after the customers. The wife's industry has made the business flourish, though her husband frequently declares his intention of selling it, in spite of her remonstrance, and in this contest he has finally prevailed, having control of the purse-strings.

The work and the anxiety during the years when the business had to be made, were very severe, and

131

during that time, this woman bore six children. If it were not for them, she would "take a dose of chloroform to-morrow!" Pain, weariness, broken rest, hard work, anxiety: these have been her unceasing portion. She declares that she would infinitely prefer death to having more children, thus unconsciously echoing the sentiment of Medea of old: "I would rather thrice stand in arms than once suffer the pangs of childbirth." She is a wounded creature, with a spoilt and shortened youth, broken nerves, and with little to look forward to but further toil.[1]

Whatever may be her feelings, she has to appear cheerful, for her husband hates to see her ailing, and she always does her utmost to please him. At her worst miseries he laughs. What is so common, he feels, cannot be very severe! She knows that she is wholly dependent on this man; that though she works hard for her living, she is without a penny in the world that she can call her own. With or without cause, she lives in a state of incessant dread that he may tire of her, as he did of his business, and leave her and the children penniless. Probably her fears are groundless, but that they are even possible marks her dependent state. Her anxiety makes her over-watchful and suspicious; she is miserable if he stays out an hour later than usual; she is jealous, and in perpetual fear of his being led away by other women. Thus her fears help to bring about their own fulfilment, for this conduct is naturally very irritating to the husband.

Perhaps there would be less unhappiness if the woman ceased to feel the injustice of her lot. But if she did so, she would sink in the scale of humanity; she would lose her self-respect. At present she feels it

---

[1] The common contention that the woman is abnormally weak who suffers in this way, is not borne out in this case. She began life in perfect health and buoyant spirits. The marvel is that any creature born of woman *can* so begin it !

keenly. Is it fair, she asks, that she should be claimed body and soul for a life-time, that she should work hard and suffer severely, without earning so much as a bare subsistence? Were she not the man's wife, he would pay her a salary for far less toil, and she would be a free agent into the bargain. She seems vaguely to hanker after the cook's place in her own establishment!

It is not a little remarkable that the present position of the married woman corresponds, in outward features, with that of a slave in early ages. In an article in an old number of the *Quarterly Review* (December 1823) the beginnings of the institution of slavery are traced to the custom of retaining prisoners of war as bondsmen, instead of killing them, in accordance with the older usage, when agriculture was in its infancy.

" In an early state of society," says the writer, " an agreement to serve is understood to be for life, and as the equivalent given (maintenance) forms apparently a slight sacrifice on the part of the master, it seems equitable to purchase such service by a payment to the parent or whoever has defrayed the expenses of infancy and education."

In return for maintenance and the sum paid for his possession, the bondsman surrenders himself, with all his service, for life, and gives up his liberty. He may be well treated, well lodged and fed, but his toil brings with it no right to self-direction or hope of respite, should the conditions of his lot prove painful. This constitutes the real difference between freedom and slavery. To be maintained, however luxuriously, without earning anything over which there is undisputed control, is to be, in so far, in the position of a slave. Other conditions may, indeed, be very unlike those of servitude, but such a situation presents its essential features. It will be seen that the married woman is exactly in this position, inasmuch as her work in the home does not procure her independence. She is the working partner in a firm in whose profits she has no share. Her share is only in

the labour.   Yet her husband imagines that he is supporting her !

Whence has arisen among good men, the state of conscience which approves this injustice ?   Many changes
must take place before it can be entirely removed; but
it is important to recognise the wrong, and to seek to
eradicate the false ideas on which it rests.

Were it possible for a wife to leave her husband without penalty, if the worst came to the worst, that worst,
in nine cases out of ten, would never come.   One seldom
hears of very bad cases of ill-treatment, when a woman
has private means under her own control.   Wives who
have begun their married life without such means, and
acquired them afterwards, notice that a marked difference
is discernible in the husband's attitude towards them.
It is the unconscious recognition of the new status.[1]

Dependence, in short, is the curse of our marriages, of
our homes, and of our children, who are born of women
who are not free—not free even to refuse to bear them.
It would be interesting, though probably not a little
painful, if we could learn what proportion of children
enter the world, whose mothers are perfectly willing and
able to bear them : willing, in a strict sense, apart from
all considerations of duty, or fear of harbouring un-
sanctioned feelings.   A true answer to this question
would shake down many brave edifices of sentiment
which are now flying holiday flags from their battle-
ments.

Nervous exhaustion and many painful forms of ill-
health among women are appallingly common, and people
try to find roundabout explanations for the fact.   Do we
need explanations ?   The gardener takes care that his
very peach-trees and rose-bushes shall not be weakened

---

[1] In one singular case of this kind, the relations between the couple had
been happy and friendly from the beginning, and the wife thought she
was far from having anything to complain of.   Yet even she noticed a
startling change of attitude after she became the possessor of a small
income, which gave her a position of independence.

by over-production (though to produce is *their* sole mission). Valuable animals are spared in the same way and for the same reason. It is only women for whom there is no mercy. In them the faculties are discouraged which lead away from the domestic " sphere." The whole nature is subjected to hot-house cultivation, in such a manner, as to drive all the vital forces in one sole direction. Such treatment means over-wrought nerves, over-stimulated instincts, weakened constitution, a low intellectual development, or, if otherwise, a development which is apt to be acquired (under the present unfavourable conditions) at the cost of farther physical suffering. And when this last calamity *does* take place, there is a general outcry against mental cultivation for women. Even men of science, who might be expected to see a little further than their noses, join in the foolish chorus : —Women will ruin their constitutions by intellectual efforts.

This misdirection of nervous energy creates innumerable miseries, and some of them seem to have become chronic, or hereditary, and from being so common have lost the very name of disease. Yet with these facts before them, people still dare to infer, from the present condition of women, their eternal limitations of function ; they still fail to see that to found a theory of society upon hereditary adaptations which they now find in a long enslaved and abused race, is to found a theory of nature upon artificial and diseased development.

The nervous strain which the civilised woman endures is truly appalling. The savage, to whom the infinite anxieties of modern life are unknown, has also the advantage of a far less severe tax on her strength, as regards her maternal functions. Nature appears to be kind to her primitive children ; their families rarely exceed two or three in number, and the task of bearing and rearing cannot be compared, for severity, to that of the civilised mother. It is a well-known fact, that a more protected, well-fed, complex life, causes the race to become more prolific, thus simultaneously increasing the demands on the nervous energy from every side. People are beginning to feel the danger of all this; but how do they propose to meet it ?   By trying to hold women back from the full possession of life, by bidding them, for heaven's sake, keep solely to their maternal functions !   One-half of the race, in short, is to be rescued at the expense of the other.   Strange as it may appear, men of science have advocated this singular method of averting the danger of race degeneration.   Women, who already are crippled in body and mind by excessive performance of the duties of maternity, are to plunge yet further in the same disastrous direction ; to cut off all chance of relief, all hope of the over-taxed system righting itself by more general distribution of energy.   The longing, so striking among the present generation, for a more healthily-balanced life must be sternly checked.   Do we not see that the mother of half a dozen children, who struggles to cultivate her faculties, nearly always breaks down under the burden ?   This naturally scares the scientific imagination, and the decree goes forth : " Cease this unwomanly effort to be human ; confine yourself to the useful animal office which Nature ordains for you. Consider the welfare of the race."   It is forgotten that this very counsel has been dinned into feminine ears for endless generations, and that the counsel has brought them   and   their   descendants   little   but   wrong   and misery.

It is a hideous ideal that we have set up for our women, and the world is wretched because they have followed it too faithfully.   An interval now of keener suffering, if it must be, on the way to freedom, would be a kinder potion for this sick world than another century of " womanly " duty and virtue, in the old pitiful sense of these terms.   Happily, there is no necessity to pass through such a terrible ordeal.   The Anglo-Saxon race is not naturally addicted to " ideas," but it prefers them, if the worst comes to the worst, to revolutionary changes. It is the women of the race who are now presenting the remedial " ideas " which taste so bitter to their generation. Although much suffering is caused by the present attempt to do the old duties more perfectly than before, while adding to them a vast number of fresh responsibilities, yet the result, in the long run, promises to be the creation of a new balance of power, of many varieties of feminine character and aptitude, and, through the consequent influx of new activities, a social revolution, reaching in its results almost beyond the regions of prophecy.

PART II

MARRIED LIFE, PRESENT AND FUTURE

" It is not true that in all voluntary association between two people one of them must be absolute master ; still less that the law shall determine which of them it shall be."—J. S. MILL.

" When we consider how vast is the number of men in any great country who are little higher than brutes, and that this never prevents them from being able through the law of marriage to obtain a victim, the breadth and depth of human misery caused in this shape alone by the abuse of the institution swells to something appalling."—J. S. MILL.

THE two essential attributes of marriage as it now stands, are the wife's dependence, economic and social, and the supposed duty to produce as many children as Fate may decide.[1] Take away from it these two solid props, and marriage, as we have hitherto understood it, ceases to exist. It is not recognised that what makes the " holy estate " so firm and inflexible is its atrocious injustice. Suppose an opponent to grant this, for the sake of argument, would he leave standing the institution, thus supported ? Injustice that has not realised itself is one thing ; injustice that is wide-awake, cool, and deliberate is quite another. Under the first we can painfully struggle on, but the last, nationally speaking, is suicidal.

This brings us to the crux of the question : Is it safe for society to permit men and women to have fair play in their mutual relations ? Is it safe to found our State upon liberty and justice ? Dare we substitute a broad and free ideal of the womanly character for a cramped and petty one ? Dare we take from marriage its barbaric elements, so that a married woman may be able to look her position frankly in the face, without resort to

---

[1] See preceding Article.

subterfuge in order to preserve her self-respect ? I go so far as to assert that no clear-headed woman can do that now without vitiating her judgment.

It ought not to be necessary, but perhaps it will be well to remind the reader, once more, that no sweeping attack upon every individual union is intended, and that a wife is not referred to as a degraded being. It is the abstract nature of the position, as legally and generally understood, to which allusion is made. An ideal marriage is possible, and indeed even now exists, in an increasing number of cases, *in spite of* the conditions alluded to above ; and such a union appears under the name of marriage, though every trace of the old patriarchal and purchase system has vanished, and therefore it is not marriage in the sense which I am criticising.

If any adventurous wife thinks that she *can* look her position approvingly in the face,[1] let her try to answer the arguments of Guido Franceschini in " The Ring and the Book," when he is pleading before the court, urging that he had acted strictly within his marriage rights in matters wherein he had been blamed by public sentiment—nay, by the august judges themselves—and that the court, which upheld in all severity the gist and meaning of marriage, had no right whatever to call him to account. Nor had it. To do so was like giving permissions to a child, and then scolding him because he availed himself of them. Listen to him, how he cuts through the crust of pretty sentiment, and lets his knife grate harsh and straight on the skeleton fact. He has been remonstrated with for the manner of his marriage. Are flesh and blood a ware ? Are heart and soul a chattel ? cry the public, who have some sentiment. To which Guido Franceschini replies :—

[1] That is, her legal and social position, as distinct from what may perhaps be her real position, in consequence of private agreement and harmony between herself and her husband. See p. 144.

> " Softly, Sirs !
> Will the Court of its charity teach poor me,
> Anxious to learn, of any way i' the world,
> Allowed by custom and convenience, save
> This same which, taught from my youth up, I trod ?
> Take me along with you ; where was the wrong step ?
> If what I gave in barter, style and state,
> And all that hangs to Franceschinihood,
> Were worthless—why, society goes to ground,
> Its rules are idiots' rambling.   Honour of birth—
> If the thing has no value, cannot buy
> Something of value of another sort,
> You've no reward or punishment to give
> I' the giving or the taking honour : straight
> Your social fabric, pinnacle to base,
> Comes down a-clatter like a house of cards.
>
>   I thought
> To deal o' the square : others find fault it seems."

" But," urge the critics:—

> " Purchase and sale being thus so plain a point,
> How of a certain soul bound up, may be,
> I' the barter with the body and money-bags ?
> From the bride's soul what is it you expect ? "

To which Guido returns :—

> " Why, loyalty and obedience—wish and will
> To settle and suit her fresh and plastic mind
> To the loyal, not disadvantageous mould ! "

Here we see Guido claiming, as his right, that which
the immemorial submission of wives has accorded and
caused to become the expected perquisite of husbands.
The law gives no definite claim here in black and white,
but usage grants a right at least as strong.

Guido goes on:—

> " With a wife I look to find all wifeliness,
> As when I buy, timber and twig, a tree—
> I buy the song of the nightingale inside :
>   Such was the pact :—Pompilia from the first
> Broke it."

Some one has suggested that perhaps Pompilia, on her
side, expected love from her husband.   There is a right
of usage here also.   To which he replies that they are
talking of marriage, not of love :—

> " The everyday conditions and no more :
> Where do these bind me to bestow one drop
> Of blood shall dye my wife's true love-knot pink ?
> Pompilia was no pigeon
>
>   but a hawk
> I bought at a hawk's price, and carried home
> To do hawk's service—at the Rotunda, say,
> Where, six o' the callow nestlings in a row,
> You pick and choose and pay the price for such.
> I have paid my pound, await my penny's worth,
> So hoodwink, starve, and properly train my bird,
> And should she prove a laggard—twist her neck !
> Did I not pay my name and style, my hope
> And trust, my all ?   Through spending these amiss
> I am here !   'Tis scarce the gravity of the court
> Will blame me that I never piped a tune,
> Treated my falcon-gentle like my finch.
> The obligation I incurred was just
> To practise mastery, prove my mastership :—
> Pompilia's duty was—submit herself,
> Afford me pleasure, perhaps cure my bile.
> And I to teach my lords what marriage means,
> What God ordains thereby, and man fulfils
> Who, docile to the dictate, treads the house."

Guido has the right on his side ; no one can gainsay
him who holds to the canon.   Marriage, with its but-
tresses of law, religion, usage, grants him all he asks.
Not one jot nor one tittle dare we deny him, and remain
of the faithful.   He may be urged to forego his privilege,
to be merciful—even that is a dangerous admission of
fallibility—but the claim is undeniable.   By the law
of the land, by the service of the Church, by all that we
cling to and uphold in the existing order of society,
Guido Franceschini is supported in his demands.   Few

people will face that truth ; few have the courage to stick to their colours ; they are so very ugly in the full sunlight. It is preferable to drape one's idol in sentiments, vague but very lofty, the loftier the better ; for they may console Pompilia, who lies crushed beneath the weight of the social order. It may soothe her immensely to know that those who support it, and all that appertains thereto—for sundry things one does not like to speak about, incidentally accompany the triumphal procession —it may, I say, console Pompilia very much to know that those who organise the triumph have sentiments that would, in sooth, do honour to a brood of callow angels !

This is not a mere form of speech. It is a simple truth, that the ugly skeleton of fact in the edifice that we call society, above all, in the institution which is said to hold it together, is kept out of sight by an overgrowth of sentiment, and we are so taken up in admiring the pleasing details of this ornamental vegetation, that we do not consider the frame on which it grows. That few people *do* know what they are supporting is evident from their disapproval of husbands as logical as Guido Franceschini. The vegetation confuses them !

What business have they to criticise the man who simply claims what his indulgent country offers ? The marriage cultus would have a short life without its unconscious heretics ! An outbreak of Guido Franceschinis would strain its timbers ruthlessly.

If the progress of society gradually raises women to independence, releasing them from the curse of unwilling motherhood, and from that of overwrought maternal instinct (a far cry still, I admit), we shall have a totally different kind of people to deal with from the men and women of to-day. The elements of human nature will remain, but their *proportions* and *relations* will be altered. And this, to all intents and purposes, is to alter human nature itself. What ideal, then, can be held impossible?

A little girl, of evidently advanced views, was once heard to enquire with bitterness : " What is the use of being a citizen of a free country if one has to be tyrannised over by one's nurse ?" Her elders were all immensely delighted and amused by the remark. Yet each of them might with justice have expressed a similar sentiment : What is the use of being a citizen of a free country if one has to be tyrannised over by one's family ?

There is, perhaps, no more difficult relation in the world than that of husband and wife. Peace is not so very hard to achieve, nor an apparent smoothness that passes for harmony. The really rare thing is a unity which is not purchased at the expense of one or other of the partners. The old notion that the man ought to be the commander, because one must have a head in every commonwealth, is a truly comic solution of the difficulty.[1] To preserve peace by disabling one of the combatants is a method that is naïve in its injustice. Where, one feels inclined to ask, again and again, in considering this whole question, is man's sense of humour? It is this sort of " peace " in the home

---

[1] The patriarchal power (among the Aryan family groups) extends over the life and liberty of the members of the family. The wife and children are absolutely in the power of the head of the family, and he has not to give account for any of his actions. We saw that the Brazilian community was constructed on these lines, which afford the typical form of brute force.—"The Primitive Family," Starcke. It is this "typical form of brute force " which survives in our own idea of the necessity for a " head " in every family.

" Elle (la loi civile) declare la femme mineure pour toujours et prononce sur elle une eternelle interdiction. L'homme est constitué son tuteur, mais s'il s'agit des fautes qu'elle peut commettre, des peines qu'elle peut subir, elle est traitee comme majeure, tout a fait responsable, et tres-severement. C'est du reste la contradiction de toutes les lois barbares. Elle est livree comme une chose, punie comme une personne."— " L'Amour," Michelet.

which brings with it the sad disenchantment that is so fatally common.

The husband's sense of power over his wife causes her to become less attractive to him, and it is this loss of attraction, *observed apart from its cause,* which creates so much fear of the effects of greater marital freedom. Ardent upholders of the present status point out that men would leave their wives without hesitation if they could, a curious admission that most marriages hold together by law rather than by affection.

What could possibly be more fatal to the wife's continued influence over her husband than the fact that she is his absolutely and for ever, quite irrespective of her wishes or of his conduct? He marries expecting exorbitantly. If the wife does not give him all he expects, he is disappointed and angry; if she *does* give it—well, it is only her duty, and he ceases to value it. It becomes a matter of course, and the romance and interest die out. The same thing in a lesser degree happens to the wife. She, too, may make vast claims upon her husband, curtail his liberty of action, and even of thought; she may drag him about with her, on the absurd assumption that it is not " united " in husbands and wives to have independent pursuits ; she may even ruin a great talent, and fritter away an otherwise useful life, through her exactions.

Often, indeed, the claims on both sides are willingly recognised, but that saves neither of the pair from the narrow influences of such a walled-in existence. Marriages of this kind are making life, as a whole, airless and lacking in vitality ; social intercourse is checked, the flow of thought is retarded ; and these unions have also the very evil effect of cutting off, in a great measure, both the husband and wife from friendly relations with others. The complaint among friends is universal : when a man or woman marries a great curtain seems to fall. As human beings they have both lost their position; they are more or less shut away in their little circle, and all the rest of the world is emphatically outside. As society is made up, to a large extent, of married couples—all tending to this self-satisfied isolation amidst undisturbed family prejudice—it suffers from a sort of coagulating process, whose effects we are all feeling in a thousand unsuspected ways. Life is tied up into myriads of tight little knots, and the blood cannot flow through the body politic. Ordinary social intercourse does little or nothing to loosen this stricture. The marital relationship of claims and restraints is, perhaps, in its vaunted " success," more melancholy than in its admitted failure.

The future offers us a very different prospect. That which was formerly a right will transform itself into an aggression; claims will become impossible, while women will no longer have to choose between freedom and the affections of the home—now the stern alternatives. The husband and wife of the future will no more think of demanding subordination, on the one side or the other, than a couple of friends who had elected to live together would mutually demand it. That, after all, is the true test. In love, there ought to be *at least* as much respect for individuality and freedom as in friendship. Love may add to this essential foundation what it pleases; but to attempt to raise further structures without this as a basis, is to build for oneself a castle in the air. It cannot last, and it does not deserve to last. A true human relationship can never be built up on mutual disrespect for personal freedom, however deep may be the affection which serves as an excuse for the aggression. The more intensely mankind learns to feel its unity, its coherence, the more deep must be the reverence for each individual nature. Stolid peace, but not living harmony, is possible without it. The truest socialism means, in this sense, the apotheosis of individualism. Under our present popular ideas, there is something terribly disappointing in marriage, even to those who start with the highest resolutions. Human nature is too severely tried. It finds itself in possession of almost irresponsible power. Its claims (by supposition just) are innumerable; there is scarcely a moment in the life of husband or wife which cannot be brought to judgment. How is it possible for two people to satisfy one another, in every word and look and deed? How can one of them invariably fit every detail of conduct to the preconceptions of the other, affected as each must be always by moods, health, chance influences, and hereditary feelings? It is mere insanity, as well as a piece of intolerable impertinence to expect it. We do not ask our friends to shape their conduct always according to our opinion, or, if we do, we are probably told to mind our own business. Neither ought those who are married, and (presumably) anxious to be mutually helpful, to lay this terrible burden on one another.

How often is the courtesy and respect which is instinctively given to a mere acquaintance, withheld from the husband or the wife! Roughness, lack of refinement in thought or word, which often disfigure this relationship, have much to do with the passing away of the first love and enthusiasm, the first so-called illusion, which was no illusion, but the beautiful flower of life's poetry, cruelly crushed under foot. The marriage relationship can never exist in its finest form until the wife can say to the husband what the heroine of Tchernuiskevsky's novel says to the man who has given her real freedom in marrying her : " Sasha, how greatly your love supports me! Through it I am becoming independent; I am getting independent even of you!"[1] Such an ideal may be held by the few, spreading gradually to the many, long before legal freedom is

[1] "A Vital Question ; or, What is to be Done?" By N. G. Tchernuiskevsky.

attained or even attempted, and this ideal makes that
freedom at once necessary and safe.

Now the question is : Must all these popular claims
and aggressions in family life continue to be suffered in
deference to a rigid convention, which, we are assured,
the nature of mankind makes necessary ?   Is the
licentious element in society to be a perpetual stum-
bling-block, causing life to crystallise into hard patterns,
separating people into inexorable groups ?   This is what
happens as an accompaniment to our supposed precautions against disorder.[1]

It was once thought impossible to bring up children
without perpetual chastisement.   This idea has been
found to be false.   Not only does it fail to restrain, but
it excites every evil impulse, and an inclination to
repeat the transgression, if possible, without being
found out.   Adult natures are no doubt more complex
than children's, but experience tends to show that
coercion acts upon them very much in the same
manner as it acts upon their juniors.   Does licentious-
ness indicate a state of physical and mental health,
or of disease ?   If a state of disease, is it incurable ?
What serious attempts have we ever made to cope with
this dangerous force ?   We destroy a thousand possible
joys, shadow the lives of harmless people, set apart
a great body of women for a purpose which we
account disgraceful — and, strange to say, we make
them no apology for our conduct, we only heap in-

[1] "So long as the legislature determines to consider adultery the only
ground for divorce, and attempts to place ' by law ' a stigma on certain
conduct and certain acts, so long our marriage laws will continue in a
vicious circle."—" Marriage and Divorce," *Fortnightly Review*, George
H. Lewes, May 1, 1885.   " Yet our divorce court to-day is as savage
and barbarous an institution ethically as the fixing up on spikes of the
heads of criminals was in the old days on London Bridge."

sults upon them—but what do we do to conquer this tyrant ?[1] Our one idea is restraint and punishment. More liberty would mean less license. " She who escapeth safe and unpolluted from out the schoole of freedome, giveth more confidence of hirself than she who commeth sound out of the school of severity and restraint," is a saying of Montaigne.

But practically, what is to be done ? How would a freer system work ? We must face the unpalatable fact, that a cut-and-dried scheme which will now seem plausible, is just as impossible as our present state of society would have appeared to the man of the Middle Ages. All that can be done, at any given time in the world's history, is to indicate the next direction of development.[2] It is futile to say that human nature is incapable of this or that, since human nature is precisely the author and creator of all the changes that the world has ever seen or ever *will* see. I have suggested that the instinctive side of human nature may be reduced to more manageable proportions ;[3] and this is surely not an entirely vain hope, unless it is also vain to hope to bring men and women into better conditions of mind and body ; unless it is vain to hope that thought and will count for something in human destiny.

It is clear that, in proportion as a life is free and rich in occupation and interest, the less temptation there will be to drown misery or chase away dulness by merely sensual pleasures. Once more, I must repeat that to demand what would appear to be an *immediately* workable system under the new conditions, is as unreasonable as it would be to ask a cattle-lifting clan of the Middle Ages to turn over a new leaf, and earn their living on the Stock Exchange. Both conceptions of existence are, however, possible and workable, and both are

[1] See " Phases of Human Development," Part III.

[2] For further treatment of this part of the subject, see ''The Future of the Home," p. 115.

[3] See ''Phases of Human Development," Part III., p. 221.

the outcome of that most plastic material—human nature.

It would indeed be easy enough to suggest general outlines of a social system in which marriage should be free, but its workability entirely depends upon whether humanity is going to educate itself in that direction. At present our education is exactly in the opposite direction. The average person of orthodox views tends to make freedom more impossible. Love, as we have seen, now comes with a vast bundle of claims in her hand, and she even passes on these claims to mere kinship, which presses them with the persistency of a Shylock. Freedom in marriage is not for those who understand freedom no better than this. When we have overcome the spirit of jealous exaction, we shall find that our whole moral ideal has undergone a profound modification. A glimpse of the end of the twentieth century might puzzle even those who are most prepared for change.[1]

---

[1] "The sense of duty is not the highest moral principle, and not only does it seem that it will undergo purification or such modification as will replace it by a higher conception, but the process has already begun. The ground of the defect of duty lies in what has been already noticed, that it conceals the spontaneity of morality. It leaves out of sight that morality is the direction in which the individual naturally moves ; what is the natural direction having been determined by eliminating all other ideas."—" Moral Order and Progress " (Alexander).

PART III

CHILDREN OF THE FUTURE

" We are educators . . . each adult generation exhales an atmosphere, moral,
intellectual, and emotional, which the juvenile generation inhales, . . . and
. . . forms into the noble or ignoble Humanity of the future."—JANE HUME
CLAPPERTON.

THE doubt and anxiety which people feel with regard to
the probable fate of the children under freer conditions,
ought to be transferred to their present state. If only for
their sakes, the present marriage system stands condemned.

The very existence of a large proportion of our children is a wrong to them and to their mothers ; the continued union of their parents is another wrong, and the
popular mode of training, dependent on existing ideals, is
yet a third.

Under a freer system, the responsibility of parents
would be more deeply felt than it can possibly be at
present, when a human creature is turned loose upon
the world as one might turn out a horse to grass. Freedom, more than anything else, fosters the sense of
responsibility.[1] The very housemaid ceases to feel responsible if her mistress watches her every minute of
the day.

It is remarkable that even the one function to which a
whole sex is asked to devote itself is, and must be, under the
old order, very badly performed. Among men we have
had division of labour ; among women such a thing has

---

[1] In Germany, divorce is allowed for incompatibility of temper, yet
there are rather fewer divorces in that country than with us. In Ibsen's
" Lady from the Sea," he depicts the morbid desires and uneasy longings
created by a state of bondage, however good and amiable may be the
person who holds the power. At the close of the play we see the wholesome, steadying effect of freedom.

scarcely existed. We give the heads of our pins into the hands of specialists ; the future race may be looked after by unqualified amateurs. This is a subject which is usually slurred over; therefore it is well to look it steadily in the face. I do not hesitate to say that every fifth or sixth child born in a family, however wealthy the family, is a deeply injured being. Indeed, in most instances, the case might be put much more strongly. We are so accustomed to a low standard of physical and mental power, that few of us recognise the mischief that has been done, unless the child has fits or rickets, and even then, there is a lurking consolatory suspicion that he has them by the grace of God. Nobody counts the miseries caused by a low vitality, by an untoward start on the race of life, by the consequences of a lack of that intelligent care which the most devoted mother in the world cannot give, if she has half-a-dozen other claimants to give it to, and no time or strength or heart to acquire the knowledge that must precede it. When shall we shake off the old and fatal notion that maternal love makes up for the lack of common-sense ?

The State must, when necessary, protect its helpless members against neglect and ill-treatment; and the free State of the future may justly demand of the parents that they shall support and educate their children, seeing that they have, without compulsion of law, or tyranny of popular sentiment, brought them into the world. But surely, in order to provide for the exceptional cases in which neglect might happen, it is not necessary to hold an entire people in bondage. This method reminds one of the policy of people who keep their whole family in unventilated rooms, because now and then somebody, in a weak state of health, might take cold from an open window. The ordinary, every-day, necessary good is sacrificed in order to guard against the possibility of an exceptional evil. It is surely childish to suppose that people in a free society, who had full opportunity of forming suitable unions, and who had willingly incurred the responsibility of children, would be perpetually breaking these ties, snapping all associations and affections, and flying off to other partners. There would be a public opinion then, as now, that would discourage such tendencies.

Granted, however, for the sake of argument, that a larger number of couples separated than is now the case. Remembering the altered conditions that are implied by the freedom to separate, can we suppose that any serious evil would result? Would the children really benefit by the continued union of parents who are pining to live anywhere but under the same roof? Moreover, be it observed, children need not necessarily be *entirely* separated from either parent (under present conditions, school-life separates them during the greater part of the year from *both*), nor need they suffer more than is unavoidable in every case where parents are not completely at one. The difficulties are almost entirely imaginary, and they take their very shaky stand on the assumption that the father and mother both have a large and constant part in their children's training.

I have elsewhere stated, at length, why it seems to me that the mother has a moral right to final authority over her children, so I will not touch upon this unpopular point here. The mother should be able to claim her children, if she desires to exercise her rights to the full; and under new economic conditions, she would have no difficulty in supporting the one or two that she would be likely to have. More often, perhaps, some compromise would be made. Separation of children and parents is now *invariably* necessary, through the practice of depriving the former of home influence during the most susceptible time of their lives. This separation, therefore, is clearly *not* looked upon as a dire calamity by the majority of parents. Boys are plunged suddenly, without guide or compass, into an entirely new world, for whose difficulties they are generally unprepared ; and Providence must decree what influences shall prevail upon the unformed spirit. Yet nobody objects, nobody says : " How sad for those boys to be deprived of the joint-guardianship of father and mother ! How distressing that the parents are not able to watch over their welfare ! "

If parental care from both sides is so essential, why is this system of exile from home not condemned ? If it is *not* essential, why is there so much horror at the idea of a partial separation from *one* of the parents in the exceptional case of a divorce ? To sacrifice the man and woman for the sake of providing the children with a constant supply of parents, no matter what may be the reluctance of the parents, is as unjust as it is inexpedient. It is strange that no one shows the smallest dismay at the sad plight of the child in the ordinary " happy home." Few people realise how much avoidable pain, and how much weakness and ill-health is traceable to the absurd traditional modes of treating infants and children. It is impossible to go into the nursery of an average Christian household, without being struck by the extraordinary ignorance there displayed of the simplest laws of hygiene, physical, mental, and moral. The child is the victim of ideas which date from the dark ages ; indeed, it would scarcely be exaggeration to say from times pre-historic. One ignorant nurse hands them on to another, and the whole race is brought up in a manner that offends, not merely scientific acumen, but the simplest common-sense. And in moral and intellectual training, the same disastrous ignorance is steadily at work, in ninety-nine homes out of a hundred—ruining the mental calibre, battering down every trace of originality, and reducing the character to a mere tame echo of conventional sentiments. The aggressive instincts of boys are

K

left unchecked, nay, assiduously cultivated; while the poor little girls learn those lessons of abject self-suppression which are to prepare them for the long chain of renunciations that stretches before them.   Would that we could place above all the copybook precepts of the Seminary for Young Ladies, Professor Clifford's aphorism : " There is one thing worse than the desire to command, and that is—the will to obey."   Montaigne is disposed to encourage women to " refuse the rules of life prescribed to the world, forasmuch as only men have established them without their consent."

There is not sufficient ground in experience for believing that the mother and father are certain, or even likely, to be the best trainers for their children.   Parenthood does *not* miraculously bestow the genius for education, nor the wide knowledge necessary for the task.   Surely, it cannot be denied that the average mother is totally unfitted for the training of mind or character.   How many women, according to popular notions, make good stepmothers ?   Yet no woman who has so little sense of justice as to treat children less kindly because they are not her own, is fit to bring up children at all.   There is, indeed, no reason for surprise that the ordinary mother should not understand principles whose application demands time and study, only possible to bestow on the business of one's life ; but that is exactly why she does her children a wrong in attempting to do for them that which she is unable to do thoroughly.   Surely they have a claim to enjoy the best training that the conditions of their century can offer.   And such training can only be provided by those who have a natural gift for the work.   Some people— but they are very few—are born with a strong influence over young minds, and a gift for attracting their love and confidence.   But these gifts of nature must be developed and supplemented by a thorough knowledge

of the laws of health, and of mental and moral development, before the tremendous responsibility ought to
be undertaken, even by such heaven-born friends of
children.[1] Nature, be it remembered, takes no count
of *motive* ; a child suffers just as much from the
mistakes of a devoted mother, as it suffers from wilful
ill-treatment.

We ought to consider, also, the enormous amount of
energy that would be set free, in our homes, by this extension of the principle of the division of labour. Only
by such means, really excellent work is possible. The
best training, therefore, is only to be achieved by breaking down our old idea that the mother should always
take charge of her child, or rather, that she should not
allow one more competent than herself to do so. Some
one *less* competent, as, for instance, the average nurse-
maid—who has not even maternal affection as a motive
for good treatment—is not objected to by popular
feeling.[2]

Some day, a mother's affection will show itself, not in

[1] Fourier hit upon a profound truth, when he placed at the foundation
of his social system the "attractions passionées" of its members. Are
there not many women among the hordes that now have to make their
own living, who would feel this "passionate attraction" to the work of
sympathetic education (it is more than "education" in the usual accepta-
tion of the word)? And could they not be trained, perhaps by means of
a college, to this important task, which no one but those really fitted by
nature and education ought to dream of undertaking?

[2] It is fully admitted that the mother is at present practically forced
to be satisfied with incompetent substitutes ; her duties compel it ; but
that is exactly what calls for reform. How many Anglo-Indians, for
instance, obliged to leave their children in England, would be thankful
if there existed, all through the country, establishments under the care
of educated, high-minded women, where children, however young, might
be left, with the certainty that the best training which the most advanced
knowledge of the century afforded, would be theirs.

When the mother in a family of moderate income is no longer head-
nurse, children's governess, and general attendant, as well as housekeeper
and performer of social duties, she would have time to make herself
efficient in her various pursuits, so that home influences would be far
more worth having than they generally are at present.

industrious self-sacrifice, which reduces her to a pulpy nonentity, feeble in body and mind, and generally ends in bringing her child to a similar condition ; but in a resolve to take the full advantage of all that science is busily providing, for those who will accept her bounties. The mother will recognise, at the same time, that self-immolation is obsolete, even among Indian widows ; and that, as a civilised human being, she is acting immorally when she voluntarily permits herself—a unit of society —to degenerate in mind or body.

Thus the aspect of a woman's duty changes, as she learns at last to understand the prophetic saying of Emerson—" We shall one day learn to supersede politics by education."

A DEFENCE OF THE "WILD WOMEN"

A DEFENCE OF THE "WILD WOMEN"

" What a great deal of trouble it would save the human race if once and for ever the predominant male would wake up to see that he has no more right to say what a woman shall or shall not do than a woman has to say what a man shall or shall not do."—ANON.

THE first impulse of women whom Mrs Lynn Linton calls "wild," is, probably, to contradict the charges that she makes against them in the course of three ruthless articles in the *Nineteenth Century;* but reflection shows the futility as well as the inconsequence of such a proceeding. After all, those who have lost faith in the old doctrines are not so much concerned to prove themselves, as individuals, wise and estimable, as to lead thinking men and women to consider popular sentiments with regard to the relation of the sexes, and to ask themselves whether the social fiat which for centuries has forced every woman, whatever be her natural inclination or powers, into one avocation, be really wise or just ; whether, in truth, it be in the interests of the race to deprive one half of it of all liberty of choice, to select for them their mode of existence, and to prescribe for them their very sentiments.

To the task of opposing the conclusions of Mrs Lynn Linton, her adversaries must bring considerable force and patience, and for this singular reason, that she gives them nothing to answer. One cannot easily reply to strings of accusations, levelled against the personal qualities of women who venture to hold views at variance with those at which the world arrived, at some undefined, but happy and infallible epoch in its history. The unbeliever finds himself thrown back upon the simple schoolroom form of discussion, consisting in flat contradiction persistently repeated until the energies give out. As this method

appears undignified and futile, it seems better to let
most of the charges pass in silence, commenting only on
one or two here and there.   It is of no real moment
whether Mrs Lynn Linton's unfavourable impression of
the women who differ from her in this matter, be just or
unjust. The question is simply: Are their views nearer or
farther from the truth than the doctrines from which
they dissent ?   As regards their personal qualities, it
must, in fairness, be remembered that the position of the
advocate of an unpopular cause is a very trying one.
The apostles of a new faith are generally driven, by the
perpetual fret of opposition and contempt, to some rancour or extravagance ; but such conduct merely partakes
of the frailty of human nature, and ought not to prejudice a really impartial mind against the views themselves.

Such a mind will consider principles and not persons ;
and although the absurdity of its champions may tell
against the spread of a new doctrine amongst the mass,
it certainly ought not to retard it among thinkers and
students of history, who must be well aware that the
noblest causes have not been able to command infallible advocates, nor to protect themselves from perilous
friends.

It would be interesting to make a collection from the
writings of Mrs Lynn Linton, of all the terrific charges
that she has brought against her sex, adding them up in
two columns, and placing, side by side, the numerous
couples that contradict each other.   At the end of this
sad list, one might place the simple sentence of defence,
" No, we are not ! " and although this would certainly
lack the eloquence and literary quality of Mrs Lynn
Linton's arguments, I deny that it would yield to them
in cogency.

There is nothing that is mean, paltry, ungenerous,
tasteless, or ridiculous, of which the woman who repudiates the ancient doctrines is not capable, according

to this lady; unless, indeed, they are such abject fools that they have not the energy to be knaves. The logic is stern: either a woman is a "modest violet, blooming unseen," unquestioning, uncomplaining, a patient producer of children, regardless of all costs to herself; suffering "every one's opinion to influence her mind," and "all venerable laws hallowed by time . . . to control her actions,"—either this, or a rude masculine creature, stamping over moors with a gun, that she may ape the less noble propensities of man; an adventuress who exposes herself to the dangers of travel, simply that she may advertise herself in a book on her return; a virago who desires nothing better than to destroy in others the liberty that she so loudly demands for herself.

There is, according to Mrs Lynn Linton, no medium between Griselda and a sublimated Frankenstein's monster, which we have all so often heard of and seldom seen. Mrs Lynn Linton's experience, in this respect, appears to have been ghastly. This is greatly to be regretted, for it has induced her to divide women, roughly, into two great classes: the good, beautiful, submissive, charming, noble, and wise, on the one hand; and on the other, the bad, ugly, rebellious, ill-mannered, ungenerous, foolish, and liberty-demanding. The "wild women" are like the plain and wicked sisters in a fairy tale, baleful creatures, who go about the world doing bad deeds, and oppressing innocence as it sits rocking the cradle by the fireside. It seems hard for the poor elder sisters to be told off to play this dreadful rôle, amid the hisses of the gallery; and they deserve some sympathy after all, for truly, the world offers temptations to evil courses, and innocence at the cradle can be desperately exasperating at times! It has a meek, placid, sneaky, virtuous way of getting what it wants, and making it hot and uncomfortable for unpopular elder sisters.

After all, in spite of Mrs Lynn Linton, there is no

more finished tyrant in the world than the meek sweet creature who cares nothing for her " rights," because she knows she can get all she wants by artifice; who makes a weapon of her womanhood, a sword of strength of her weakness, and does not disdain to tyrannise over men to her heart's content by an ungenerous appeal to their chivalry.   She is a woman—poor, weak, helpless, and her husband may not call his soul his own!   Tears are a stock-in-trade, and nerves a rock of defence.   She claims no rights—she can't understand what all this absurd talk is about—she is quite satisfied with things as they are.   Personal dignity she has none; it would sadly interfere with her successful methods of insinuating herself through life, in serpentine fashion.   She gets what she can as best she may, living by her wits; a mere adventuress, after all, in spite of her unblemished character; appealing to men's frailties, chivalry, as every member of a subject class has to appeal, if any great success, or even a bare livelihood is to be hoped for.

But far be it from me to affirm, in simple opposition to Mrs Lynn Linton, that all women of the old school are of this kind.   My object is not to bring a counter-charge, but to point to the type which power on the one side, and subordination on the other, tend to produce.   There are thousands, however, of the time-honoured school, who never dream of attempting this unconscious retaliation.   Many of them neither demand rights nor win their way by artifice.   They accept their lot, exactly as it is, in a literal spirit, being just enough developed to see the meanness of trading upon the chivalry of men, and not enough so to resent being placed in a position which makes them dependent, utterly and hopelessly, upon masculine favour.   These women—the most pathetic class of all—have been so well drilled to accept their position without question, that they launch their complaints only at Fate and Nature, if ever they are moved to complain at all.   Their con-

science and their generosity forbid them to make use of
the usual weapons of a dependent race : artifice and
flattery.   They are thus denied even this redress,
which less sensitive women enjoy without stint.   These
half-developed women respond loyally to the stern demands made upon them by public sentiment.   They
are martyrs to " duty " in its narrowest sense ; they
turn a meek ear to society when it addresses homilies
to them.   It does not strike them as unjust, nor do
they even enjoy the sad consolation of perceiving the
humour of the situation, when their stern monitors, in
all the pomp and circumstance of arbitrary authority,
demand of them the loftiest principles, burden them
with the heaviest responsibilities, while continuing to
deprive them of all corresponding rights.

In short, the women of the old order and the women
of the new, have faults and virtues, each after their own
kind, and it is idle to make general affirmations about
either class.

It is well, therefore, to check the inherent instinct to
contradict, when Mrs Lynn Linton says that women of
the new faith are all evil and ugly.   One must say,
rather, that this is a mere matter of opinion, formed
from the impression that each person gathers from individual experience, and from the bias with which that
experience is met.   Let, however, the impression be as
unfavourable to the " wild women " as it may, it is
neither fair nor philosophic to refuse to consider their
claims.   The liberal-minded will remember that the
claims of a class hitherto subordinate always seem preposterous, and that the more complete has been their
exclusion, the more ridiculous will appear their aspirations.   We can accurately measure their degree of
subjection by the loudness of the popular outcry against
their claims.   Yet, the inclination to treat with derision
any new demand for liberty, stands on a level with the
instinct of the street urchin to jeer at anything to which

he is unaccustomed, as, for example, any person in foreign garments, though the latter excel a thousand times, in dignity and comeliness, the natives of the country.

It is not very surprising if some of the apostles of the new faith, irritated by the most powerful hindrances of law, sentiment, tradition—baffling, subtle, unceasing as these are—have made the mistake, as I think, of seeking to emphasise their demand for the liberty that men enjoy, by imitating men's habits and manners, and by seizing every occasion to take part in the fierce battle for existence, as if that were a desirable thing in itself, instead of an unhappy necessity. They are not alone in their error, however ; they are not singular when they fail to see that the life that men now lead, in the effort to " earn a living and to succeed," is perilous to themselves and to the race. To add to that great body of struggling men, another body of struggling women would, evidently, by itself, not mend matters; and it is clear that the hopes which we may hold for the future of the race, through the emancipation of women, cannot rest on the prospect of their entering the tumultuous arena of competition. Undeniably, it would be wiser if women would use their influence to render the conflict less fierce, to slacken the greed for money, success, display, and to turn the ambitions of men to more rational and fruitful ways.

But however true all this may be, it is unluckily also true that women have to live, and that even those who possess a father or a husband have, at most, food and shelter ; they have not independence. The wife among the less prosperous of the middle classes, who takes upon her shoulders at least half the burden of the household—to put it very mildly—may toil all her life and grow worn with anxiety and worry, but she will still be as dependent upon her husband's will or caprice as if she were an idler, living upon his bounty.[1]

[1] See " Motherhood under Conditions of Dependence," p. 131.

Women are beginning to feel this, more or less distinctly,
and to desire to earn a little money for themselves, so
that they may possess some means of subsistence that is
really their own, small though it may be. This is surely
natural enough, however evil may be the consequences
of an inrush of women workers into the labour market.
Since the work of women in their homes, is not of a kind
to give them independence, they are beginning to seek
for employment of a sort that *is* recognised as deserving
of reward, knowing that their pecuniary position eternally
stands in the way of any improvement, as regards their
legal and social status, and that it often obliges them to
submit to a thousand wrongs and indignities which could
not otherwise be placed upon them.

A certain number of rebels are bending all their
energies to the removal of this invincible hindrance,
and to attain this end they are forced to join, more or
less, in the struggle for a livelihood. It will be a happy
day for humanity when a woman can stay in her own
home without sacrificing her freedom. Short-sighted is
the policy which would keep the wife and mother helpless in the hands of the man whose home she sustains
and holds together, which would give her but a meagre
share of right to the children which have cost her so
much to bear and tend, while burdening her with fullest
responsibility regarding them. To this point I would
especially call the attention of that large portion of the
community who are convinced of the importance of the
fireside and the home, who believe that in every other
locality the woman is out of her sphere. Would they
not use their influence most wisely, from their own
point of view, in seeking to remove some of the heavy
penalties that are attached to the enjoyment of home
and fireside, and to make these sanctuaries deserve a
little better all the sentiment that has been lavished
upon them ?

It is easy, indeed, to see the peril to the well-being of

the race that lies in the labour of women outside the home ; that peril can scarcely be exaggerated.   But if women demand the natural human right to take their share of the opportunities, such as they are, which the world has to offer—if they desire the privilege of independence (a privilege denied them, work as they will, within the home), by what right does society refuse their demand ?   Men are living lives and committing actions, day by day, which imperil the well-being of the race ; on what principle are women only to be restrained ?   Why this one-sided sacrifice, this artificial selection of victims for the good—or supposed good—of humanity ?   The old legends of maidens who were chosen every year, and chained to a rock on the shore, to propitiate gods or sea-monsters, seem not in the least out of date.

Sacrifices were performed more frankly in those days, and nobody tried to persuade the victims that so far from constituting a grievance, it was an enjoyable and blessed thing to be devoured.   They did not talk about " woman's sphere " to a maiden chained to a rock within sight of the monster, nor did they tell her that the " true woman " desired no other destiny.   They were brutal, but they did not add sickly sentiment to their crime against the individual.   They carried out the hideous old doctrine of vicarious sacrifice—which is haunting us like an evil spirit to this day—in all good faith and frankness, and there was no attempt to represent the monster as an engaging beast when you got to know his inner self.

Society is unjust in exacting these sacrifices ; every member of it must stand equal in its sight, if it would claim the name of a free state.   On the soil of such a state, there must be no arbitrary selection of victims for the general good, made from a certain class, or, still worse, from a certain sex.   One can imagine the heaven-assaulting howl that would go up, were it proposed to deal in this way with a particular body of men.   Loud would be the protest of this hapless band, picked out for sacrifice, should they be denied the right, common to all others, of seeking their fortunes as might seem good to them ! No argument about the welfare of the race would reconcile a nation of free-born men to such a proposal. Yet this is the argument that free-born men do not hesitate to employ, as a plea for making an arbitrary exception to the disadvantage of women.

The attempt to force upon these any sacrifice, on the sole ground of their sex ; to demand of them a special act of renunciation of rights and privileges on that account, gives us an exact analogue of the old tribute to the gods of a nation which chose its victims, not by fair hazard from the population, but from a class set apart for the iniquitous purpose. Such actions are subversive of all social life, for the existence of a community depends, finally, upon its respect for the rights of its individual members. Upon these rights society is built ; without them, nothing is possible but an aggregation of tyrants and slaves, which does not deserve the name of a society, since it is bound together by force, and the union between its members is accidental, not organic. On what rests, finally, my safety and freedom as a citizen, but on the understanding that if I leave your rights intact, you will also respect mine ?

But further : the argument which takes its stand upon the danger to the community of the freedom of women, besides being unfair (since it would select a whole sex for the propitiatory victims), is, on its own ground, fallacious. True, indeed, is it that if all women were to rush into the labour market and begin to compete with men and with one another, the result would be evil ; but it is *not* true that if they were to be placed on an equality with men in the eye of the law, if in marriage they were free from all artificial disability, if in society they had no special prejudices to contend with—it is not true in *that* case that the consequence of this change in their position

would be detrimental to the real interests of the commonwealth. On the contrary, its influence would be for good,
and for more good than perhaps anyone now dares to believe.
And among the many causes of this beneficent result we
may number this : that women would be able to choose
the work for which they were best suited. We should
have fewer governesses who loathed teaching, fewer wives
who could do most things better than look after a house,
and fewer mothers to whom the training of children was
an impossible task. Moreover, Society would rejoice in
more of that healthy variety among her members which
constitutes one of the elements of social vitality. There
is room for all kinds of women, did we but realise it ;
and there is certainly no reason why the present movement should sweep away all those of the ancient type
in whom Mrs Lynn Linton takes delight. They have
their charm, but it must be acknowledged that, for all
their meekness, nothing would please them better than
tyrannically to dictate to their less chastened sisters,
what mode of life and what kind of sentiments they
shall adopt. By what charter or authority does the
domestic woman (like the person in the train who wants
the window up) attempt to restrict, within her own
limits, women who entirely disagree with her in opinion
and in temperament ?

Granted, for the moment, that Mrs Lynn Linton and
her followers are justified of Heaven in their views, and
that it always was and always will be necessary for
women to dedicate themselves wholly to the production
of the race ; still, this truth—if such it be—must be left
to demonstrate itself without any tyranny, direct or indirect, from those who realise it ; otherwise they violate the
conditions of social liberty, and even their own principle
is jeopardised, through being forced upon the unconvinced.
The history of all persecutions, religious or other, ought
to warn us against the danger of allowing the promulga-
tion of a faith, true or false, by forcible means, and I

include among forcible means all forms of coercive prejudice and sentiment, for often these are far more powerful than legal enactments.   Let us not forget the glorious
privilege of the citizen of a free state to be in the wrong,
and to act upon his error until the torch-bearers of truth
shall be able to throw light upon his pathway.   That
once accomplished, his adherence will be worth having.

The demand that all women shall conform to a certain
model of excellence, that they shall be debarred from
following the promptings of their powers,—whatsoever be
the pretext for the restriction,—is the outcome of an
illiberal spirit, and ought to be resisted as all attacks on
liberty ought to be resisted.   The fact that the attack is
made on liberties which, as yet, are only candidates for
existence, is the sole reason why Englishmen do not
resent the aggression.

Let it be remembered, for the consolation of those who
fear the results of this new movement, that if modern
women are lapsing from the true faith, if they are really
insurgents against evolutionary human nature, instead of
being the indications of a new social development, then
their fatal error will assuredly prove itself in a very
short time.   Should some harm be suffered in the proving, that is merely the risk that has to be taken, in all
free states, in order to secure the possibility of progress.

These, then, are the principles upon which women of
the new faith claim tolerance for their views, be they
right or wrong.   Having demanded these initial rights,
they then proceed to give their reasons for holding such
views, and for the rebellion which they preach against
the old order.

To the time-honoured argument that Nature intended
man to be anything and everything that his strength of
muscle and of mind permitted, while she meant woman
to be a mother, and nothing else, the rebels reply that
if a woman has been made by nature to be a mother, so
has a cow or a sheep ; and if this maternal capacity be

L

really an infallible indication of principal function, there
is nothing to prevent this reasoning from running down-
hill to its conclusion, namely, that the nearer a woman
can become to a cow or a sheep the better.

If popular feeling objects to this conclusion, and yet
still desires all women to make maternity their chief
duty, it must find another reason for its faith, leaving
nature's sign-posts out of the question. On these sign-
posts man himself is privileged to write and re-write the
legends, though of this power he seems at present to be
unconscious, persistently denying it, even while his restless fingers are busy at their work.

This dear and cherished appeal to nature, however,
will never be abandoned by the advocates of the old
order, while breath remains to them. But if they use
the argument, they ought not to shrink from its consequences, nor, indeed, *would* they, but that it happens
that women, as a matter of fact, have by this time, in
spite of so much discouragement, risen above the stage
of simple motherhood, thus accustoming their critics to
attributes distinctively human. These newer attributes,
having become familiar, no longer seem alarming or
" unnatural." In our present stage of development, we
demand of a woman that she shall be first of all a
mother, and then that she develop those human qualities
that best harmonise with her position as such. " Be it
pleasant or unpleasant," Mrs Lynn Linton says, " it is
none the less an absolute truth—the *raison d'être* of a
woman is maternity . . . the cradle lies across the door
of the polling-booth and bars the way to the Senate."

We are brought, then, to this conclusion : that if there
be any force in what is commonly urged respecting
Nature's " intentions " with regard to woman, her development as a thinking and emotional being, beyond the
point where human qualities are superficially useful to
her children, is " unnatural " and false, a conclusion
which leads us straight away to Oriental customs and

to Oriental ethics. Moreover, another consideration con-
fronts us. Nature, besides designing women to be mothers,
designed men to be fathers : why, then, should not the
man give up his life to his family in the same wholesale
way ?   " The cases are so different," it will be said.
Yes, and the difference lies in the great suffering
and risk which fall solely to the share of the mother.
Is this a good reason for holding her, for her whole life,
to this painful task, for demanding that she shall allow
her tastes and talents to lie idle, and to die a slow and
painful death, while the father, to whom parenthood
is also indicated by " nature," is allowed the privilege
of choosing his own avocations without interference ?
Further, if woman's functions are to be determined solely
by a reference to what is called nature, how, from this
point of view, are we to deal with the fact that she
possesses a thousand emotional and intellectual attributes
that are wholly superfluous to her merely maternal
activities ?   What does Mrs Lynn Linton consider that
" nature intends " by all this ?

In the present order of society, speaking roughly, a
woman, to whom maternity seems unsatisfying or dis-
tasteful, has either to bring herself to undertake, to the
exclusion of all other interests, that one task for which
she is unfitted, or to deny her affections altogether.   To
man, the gods give both sides of the apple of life ; a
woman is sometimes permitted the choice of the halves,
—either, but not both.   In thousands of cases she is
offered neither.

Yet every new development of society, every over-
throw of ancient landmarks, tends to prove more and
more conclusively that this fetish " Nature," who is
always claimed as the patroness of the old order, just
when she is busy planning and preparing the new, has
not separated the human race into two distinct sections
with qualities entirely and eternally different.   If this
were so—if women were, in fact, the only beings under

heaven not modifiable by education and surroundings, then we should be forced to reconstruct from the foundation our notions of natural law, and to rescind the comparatively modern theory that it is unwise to expect effects without causes, or causes without effects. We should live once more in a world of haphazard and of miracle, in which only one fact could be counted upon from age to age—viz., the immutable and stereotyped " nature " of women.

Unless we are prepared for this antique and variegated creed, we cannot consistently pronounce, as Mrs Lynn Linton so authoritatively pronounces, what is the sphere or *raison d'être* of either sex, and what it must be for evermore. It seems, indeed, safe to predict that women will continue to bear children, but it is far from safe to prophesy to what extent that function will in the future absorb their energies. We know that although men have been fathers from the beginning of human history, they have not made fatherhood the key-note of their existence. On the contrary, it has been an entirely secondary consideration. They have been busy in influencing and fashioning a world which their children are to inherit—a world that would be sorrier than it is, if men had also made the fact of parenthood the central point of their career.

The disastrous consequences of such conduct on the part of women have been dwelt upon at length elsewhere in this volume.[1] It is impossible to exaggerate these evils, and impossible to insist on them too strongly, seeing the misery that springs from them, and the stubborn prejudice that still perseveres in denying their existence. The dedication of a whole sex to this exhausting function has gone far to destroy the healthy balance of the racial constitution, physical, mental, and moral. It has thrown work on to unfit shoulders, formed a sort of press-gang

---

[1] See "Motherhood under Conditions of Dependence," also "Future of the Home."

of the most terrible kind, inasmuch as unwilling motherhood is worse than unwilling military service.[1] It has
deprived the very children, on whose behalf this insane
cruelty has been wrought, of the benefit of possessing
really efficient mothers. They have been doomed to
grow up under the influence of tired-out, half-educated
women who can scarcely manage their own weary lives,
much less guide the growth of young souls and bodies
during the critical and fate-deciding years of childhood
and early youth. It may seem paradoxical, but is none
the less true, that we shall never have really good
mothers, until women cease to make motherhood the
central idea of their existence. The woman who has no
interest larger than the affairs of her children is not a
fit person to train them.

For the sake of men, women, and children, it is to be
hoped that women will come to regard motherhood with
new eyes; that the force of their artificially fostered impulses will become less violent, and that there may be
an increase in them of the distinctly *human* qualities
and emotions in relation to those that are merely maternal. It is this *change of proportion* in the force of
human qualities that virtually creates a new being, and
makes progress possible. Once more, in the light of
this truth, how false are all the inferences of phrases
such as "Nature intends," "Nature desires." She intends
and desires nothing—she is an abject slave. *Man* intends, *Man* desires, and " Nature," in the course of
centuries, learns to obey.

This worship of " Nature " is a strange survival in a
scientific age of the old image-worship of our ancestors.
She is our Freya or Hertha, a personal will who designs
and plans. This is a subtle form of superstition which
has cunningly nestled among the folds of the garment of
Science, and there it will lurk, safe and undetected, for
many years, to discourage all change, to cast discredit on

[1] See note to p. 175.

all new thought, to hold man to his errors, and to blind him to his own enormous power of development.

It is this insidious superstition that prevents intelligent people—nay, persons of scientific training—from recognising the effect upon women of their circumstances. Professions are known to leave their mark on men, although the influence of a man's profession is not so incessant and overwhelming as are the conditions of women's lives, from which there is no escape from the cradle to the grave. Yet it is always grudgingly and doubtfully admitted, if at all, that this fact offers an explanation of any bad quality in the feminine character. No one seems to realise how, age after age, women have been, one and all, engaged in the same occupations, subjected to the same kind of stimulus and training; how each individual, of infinitely varying multitudes, has been condemned to one function for the best years of life, and that function an extremely painful and exhausting one. No one seems to understand that these causes *must* produce effects, and that they have produced, among others, the effect in women of certain tyrannous and overwrought instincts, which we say, reverentially and obstinately, " Nature has implanted in woman." We might more accurately say : Suffering, moral and mental starvation, physical pain, disease induced by the over-excitement of one set of functions—these have fostered impulses which we have the assurance to call sacred.

At the present time, some very interesting researches are being carried on, which tend to show, so far as they have gone, that the constitution of women has been literally destroyed by the centuries of ill-usage, often unwitting, which public sentiment has forced them to submit to; whilst their training, in combination with their absolute dependence on men, has induced them often to endure their fate as if it were the will of Heaven. These researches show that through these ages of

overstrain of every kind—physical, emotional, nervous—
one set of faculties being in perpetual activity while the
others lay dormant, woman has fallen into a state that
is more or less ailing and diseased; that upon her
shoulders has been laid the penalty of the injustice and
selfishness of men.[1]

[1] Ellis Ethelmer, the author of a remarkable pamphlet called "Life to
Woman" (obtainable from Mrs Wolstenholme Elmy, Buxton House,
Congleton, Cheshire), brings forward evidence which proves this point.
One or two instances given may here be quoted, the reader being
reminded that an immense body of similar evidence lies behind that
which is adduced in this most interesting pamphlet.

The writer first points out how marriage has been the subject of
legislative enactments and religious ordinances, and always seemingly
with the same end in view—increasing of the population. For this
purpose, such agencies have employed "injunctions and allurements—
threats of infamy and perdition for infertility, and bribes of worldly
comfort or eternal Paradise for the begetting of a progeny." "These,"
says Ellis Ethelmer, "have been held out by rulers, spiritual and temporal, in Church or State, throughout all ages, to induce the populace
to 'increase and multiply' (that the ruler's own property and power
might be swollen in the process)." . . . Evidence on this point might
be adduced ranging from the Mosaic injunction, "increase and multiply," and the ancient Greek, Roman, and Oriental honours or civic
privileges conferred on fathers of large families, down to the modern
national or colonial bounties offered to inhabitants or immigrants simi-
larly qualified. Malthus says: "The customs of some nations, and the
prejudices of all," have acted in some degree like a bounty on the getting
of children. ("On Population," i. 8.) Inducement to propagation has
been a studied object of both religious and civil precept; appeals to
man's nobler aspiration or baser sensuality, as either seemed likely to
prove the more effective for the object in view. The patriarch of the
Jewish nation is represented as being prompted by the promise of a
progeny "as the sand which is upon the sea-shore" for multitude; and
each male scion was spurred by the assurance of wealth and happiness to
him who had his "quiver full" of children. The evident bearing of the
teaching was that the begetting of a multiplicity of children was a
religious as well as a civic duty, *to be performed even in default of
personal impulse.* This factitious and double-stringed appeal has been
played upon in a hundred different ways in the history of all nations.
Higher honours were decreed to prolific fathers by the State during life,
and greater bliss was promised them after death by the Church."

"In Corea, the male human being who is unmarried is treated with
the greatest indignity." . . .

"In India," according to the Laws of Manu, "marriage is the twelfth
Sanskara, and thus a religious duty incumbent upon all." (Wester-

Have we not gone far enough along this path of
destruction; or must women still make motherhood their
chief task, accepting the old sentiment of subservience
to man, until they drive yet further into the system
the cruel diseases that have punished the insanities of
the past; diseases which are taking vengeance upon the
victims of ill-usage for their submission, and pursuing
their children from generation to generation with relent-
less footsteps? Such is the counsel of Mrs Lynn Linton
and her school. Upon the consequences of all this past
ill-treatment is founded the pretext for women's disabilities in the present. They are physically weak,
nervous, easily unstrung, and for this reason, it is urged,
they must continue to pursue the mode of life which has
induced these evils. This is strange reasoning.

The suffering of women to-day is built upon their
suffering of yesterday and its consequences. It is surely

marck, "History of Marriage," p. 41.) The Abbé Reynal says of these
Hindu laws: "Population is made a primitive duty, so sacred a command of nature that the law permits to cheat, to lie, and to commit
perjury in trying to bring about a marriage." "According to the
Talmud, the authorities can compel a man to marry, and he who lives
single at the age of twenty is accursed by God almost as if he were a
murderer." (Westermarck, "Marriage," p. 141.)

"A Mahommedan is in some degree obliged to polygamy, from a
principle of obedience to his prophet, who makes one of the greatest
duties of man to consist in procreating children to glorify the Creator."
(Malthus, "On Population," i. 7.) "Zoroaster declared propagation
a meritorious act; enjoined multiplicity of children; made the 'obedience' of wives to their husbands a great matter of duty; and commanded that every woman should be a wife. He took a sure way to
tempt or frighten an ignorant people into propagation, by announcing
that 'children were the glory of the celestial spirits, and helped their
parents after death over the bridge that joined the heaven to the earth.'"
(Bryant Barrett, "Code Napoleon," vol. i. p. 87.)

"At Sparta, the obligation of marriage was legal, like the military
service." (Letourneau, "Evolution of Marriage," p. 195.)

Aristotle says: "A man who had three sons was exempt from the
night-watch, and he who had four enjoyed a complete immunity from
public burdens." ("De Republico," lib. ii. c. 6.)

In Roman legislation, as Alexander, the mediæval writer, summarises:
"Moreover, the old Romans bestowed Prætorships, Quæstorships, and

a rather serious matter to cut off a human being from
whatever the world has to offer him, in this short life,
even if the vocation appointed be of the most desirable.
From this point of view, what force or meaning have
Mrs Lynn Linton's taunts and accusations against her
sex, even though they were all perfectly just ?   It is
probable that women, in virtue of their susceptible
physical constitution and nervous system (a quality, by
the way, which distinguishes the man of genius from the
ordinary being) are more responsive than men are to
their surroundings. Therefore, all that Mrs Lynn Linton
says, if true, about the wildness of ignorant women in
times of excitement—she cites for an example the
tricoteuses of the French Revolution—might perhaps be
explained on this ground. A quick response to stimulus
is *not* the mark of a being low in the scale of existence,
though it may lead to extravagant deeds when untutored.

Consulships, and honours and magistracies on none but the parents of
many children." (Bk. iv. chap. 8.)

Sir P. Colquhoun ("Summary of the Roman Civil Law," par. 571,
573) says : "*Liberti* (manumitted slaves) were freed from servitude,
and freemen from the burden of tutorship, in virtue of a number of
children. The first places in the theatres were reserved to those who
exceeded in the number of their issue. Further, those who living at
Rome had three children, in Italy four, or in the provinces five, were
exempted from personal public duties."

In China : "A woman's sole chance of any happiness in a future life
is made contingent on her maternity ; though, again, in this labour a
daughter is not to count. Only as a mother of a son, as the continuator
of the direct line of a family, can a woman escape from her degradation."
(See " Woman Free," p. 68.)

In India : "To the widow of high caste a hint of the Vedic reward of
the 'world of life' is held out ; while, in lower conditions, the woman
is too much a slave for inducement (other than injunction and threat) to
be deemed of any necessity ; her bodily servitude and sexual abuse from
early youth is almost beyond belief." (See "Woman Free," p. 71 *et seq.*)

"To die in giving birth is accounted martyrdom."

In Rome, certain civic privileges were given to the mother of more
than three children. The old festivals, and many ancient religious
observances, are adduced in support of the author's contention, namely,
that there has been enormous over-stimulus on one side of the nature
and faculty.

But Mrs Lynn Linton will not look at this question philosophically. She hurls accusations at her sisters, as if it pleased her to add another and yet another insult to those which the literature of centuries—with that exquisite chivalry which we are so often warned our freedom would destroy—has never tired of flinging at the defenceless sex. It does not strike Mrs Lynn Linton to inquire into the real causes that underlie all these problems of a growing human nature; she prefers the finger of scorn, the taunt, the inexpensive sneer.

Why does she so harshly condemn the results of the system of things which she so ardently approves? If all has really been so well in the State of Denmark, how is it that women (according to her showing) have become such ridiculous and contemptible idiots, that they are to be held fitted only for the purposes of race production? To make her position more difficult to understand, Mrs Lynn Linton dwells, with some insistence, on the effects upon her sex of their training. She speaks of "ideal qualities which women have gained by a certain amount of sequestration from the madding crowd's ignoble strife. . . . Are the women at the gin-shop bar," she demands, "better than the men at the gin-shop door, the field-hands in sun-bonnets more satisfactory than those in brimless hats?" This is to prove that women have no real moral superiority. Elsewhere, however, is asked: "Can anyone point out anywhere a race of women who are superior to their conditions?" All this is strange reasoning from one who takes her stand on the fiats of "Nature," as distinguished from the influences of surroundings.

One might ask: "Can anyone point out anywhere a race of *men* who are superior to their conditions?" But this possible question never seems to strike Mrs Lynn Linton, for she exposes herself all through the article to the same form of demand, and she nowhere attempts to meet it. Her mode of warfare is indeed bewildering ; for she attacks from both sides, makes double and antagonistic use of the same facts, and she does not at all object to assertions clearly contradictory, provided they are separated in time and space by the interval of a paragraph or two.

Her arguments, when formidable, mutually and relentlessly devour each other, like so many *plus* and *minus* quantities, which, added together, become cancelled and leave a clean *zero* between them.

Unconscious, however, of this cannibalism among her legions, the authoress finds herself at the close of her article with a gigantic and robust opinion which nothing —not even her own arguments—can disturb.

As an instance of this strange suicidal tendency of her reasoning, we may compare the already quoted paragraphs, setting forth the effects of environment upon the woman's temperament, with the even more determined assertion of its eternal, unalterable, and God-ordained nature.   Confront these two statements, and what remains ?   Mrs Lynn Linton seems to half surrender her position when she says that ". . . there are few women of anything like energy or brain-power who have not felt in their own souls the ardent longing for a freer hand in life " ; but the following sentence seems to run still further into the jaws of the enemy : " Had Louis the Sixteenth had Marie Antoinette's energy and Marie Antoinette Louis's supineness, the whole story of the Reign of Terror, Marat, Charlotte Corday, and Napoleon might never have been written." What doctrine of Mrs Lynn Linton's does it even *seem* to support ?

In unblushing contradiction of this sentiment, Mrs Lynn Linton asserts that political women have always been " disastrous," and that even Mme. Roland " did more harm than good when she undertook the manipulation of forces that were too strong for her control, too vast for her comprehension."

Were the forces of the French Revolution within the

grasp of any one person, and does it tend to prove
woman's inability for any but the domestic sphere, that
Madame Roland did not stem the tide of this great
movement which had been preparing for centuries be-
forehand, and which proved intractable to many of the
sterner sex, as well as to the " disastrous " Madame
Roland ?

" Women are both more extreme and more impression-
able than men," Mrs Lynn Linton says ; " and the spirit
which made weak girls into heroines and martyrs, honest
women into the yelling *tricoteuses* of the blood-stained
saturnalia of '92, still exists in the sex, and among ourselves as elsewhere."

In short, when a " weak " girl espouses martyrdom, she
is prompted thereto by a sort of hysteria, male heroism
alone being heroic.

While admitting, nay emphasising, on the one hand, the
fact of the remodelling force of circumstances, Mrs Lynn
Linton denies that feminine character and intelligence
can ever be altered by one hairsbreadth, except—and
here comes the third and crowning contradiction—
except for the worse.

Among the many other minor points which this writer
has touched upon, are several which call for special
comment, from the point of view opposed to hers.   For
example, we are asked to believe that the peace of the
home practically depends on the political disabilities
of woman ; or, in other words, that a man is unable to
endure in his wife opinions differing from his own.   I
do not believe that men are quite so childish and petty
as all this ; but if they are, it is indeed high time that
they should learn the lesson of common courtesy and
tolerance.

The device of keeping peace between two persons, by
the disarmament of one of them, is ingenious and simple,
but there is a temptation to think that such peace as
that, if peace it can be called, would be well exchanged

for strife. Does peace, indeed, mean the stagnation that
arises from the relationship between the free and the
fettered, or does it mean the generous mutual recognition
of the right of private judgment? The denial of political
power to women, if it ever does prevent dissension,
achieves at best, on the part of the wife, unreasoning
acquiescence, and not rational agreement.

Mrs Lynn Linton says that "amongst our most re-
nowned women are some who say with their whole heart,
' I would rather have been the wife of a great man, or
the mother of a hero, than what I am—famous in my
own person.' " That is a matter of taste, but it seems
strange that these famous women should not have acted
upon their predilections. Against the following sentence
I cannot refrain from expressing a sense of revolt; but
the revolt is on behalf of men rather than of women.
" But the miserable little manikin who creeps to obscurity,
overshadowed by his wife's glory, is as pitiful in history
as contemptible in fact. The husband of the wife is no
title to honour ; and the best and dearest of our famous
women take care that this shall not be said of them and
theirs."

Are men, then, to be treated as if they were a set of
jealous schoolboys, or superannuated invalids, whom the
discreet person allows to win at chess, because they have
a childish dislike to being beaten ?

It is consoling to remember that the ideas on which
such feelings rest are giving way, slowly but surely, in
all directions. It is only when the rebellion is extended
over evidently new ground that Mrs Lynn Linton and
her followers begin to sound the tocsin, assuring the
rebellious woman that she shows " a curious inversion
of sex, disdaining the duties and limitations imposed on
her by Nature." As a crowning taunt, Mrs Lynn Linton
says : " All women are not always lovely, and the wild
women never are." This reminds one of the exasperated
retort of an angry child who has come to the end of his

invention—a galling if somewhat inconsequent attack
upon the personal appearance, which is generally the
last resort of outraged juvenile nature.

Nothing perhaps can better show the real attitude of
this lady and her followers on this question, than her
irritation against those who are trying to bring a ray of
sunlight into the harems and zenanas of the East.

" Ignorant and unreasonable," she says, " they would
carry into the sun-laden East the social conditions born
of the icy winds of the North. . . . In a country where
jealousy is as strong as death, and stronger than love,
they would incite women to revolt against the rule
of seclusion, which has been the law of the land for
centuries before we were a nation at all.   That rule has
worked well for the country, inasmuch as the chastity
of Hindu women and the purity of the family life are
notoriously intact."

If Mrs Lynn Linton approves of the relation of the
sexes in the East, and looks upon it with an eye of
fondness, because it dates back into ages whose savagery
breaks out in the blood of civilised men to this day, then
she may well set herself in opposition to the rebellion,
among modern women, against the less intolerable injustice which they suffer in the West.   Did we happen
to be living in harems in South Kensington or Mayfair,
with the sentiment of the country in favour of that
modest and womanly state of seclusion, it is easy to
imagine with what eloquence Mrs Lynn Linton would
declaim against the first hint of insurrection—although
in that case, by the way, the strictly unfeminine occupation of writing articles would be denied her.

The really grave question raised in this lady's work,
is that of the effect of the political and social freedom of
women upon the physical well-being of the race ; for while
past conditions have been evil, future ones may conceivably
be equally so, though they could with difficulty be worse.
This is, indeed, a serious problem, which will require

all the intelligence of this generation to solve. But first,
I would suggest what appears to be a new idea (strange as
this may seem), namely, that the rights of the existing race
are at least as great as those of the coming one. There
is something pathetically absurd, in the sacrifice to their
children, of generation after generation of grown people.
Who were the gainers by the incessant surrender ? Of
what avail was all that renunciation on behalf of those
potential men and women, if, on their attainment of that
degree, they too have to abandon the fruits of so much
pain, and so many lost possibilities, and to begin, all
over again, the weaving, *ad infinitum*, of this singular
Penelope's web ? The affairs of the present are carried
on by the adult population, not by the children ; and
if the generations of adults are going to renounce, age
after age, their own chances of development—resigning
opportunities of intellectual progress for the sake of
their children—how, in the name of common sense, will
they benefit humanity ? For those children also, when
their minds are ripe for progress, must, in accordance with
this noble sentiment, immediately begin, in *their* turn,
to renounce, and resign, and deny themselves, in order
to start another luckless generation upon the same
ridiculous circle of futility.

I fear that it is not unnecessary to add that I do not
here inculcate neglect of children, but merely claim some
regard for the parent whom it cost previous parents so
much to bear, and rear, and train. I protest against
this insane waste of human energy, this perpetual
renunciation for a race that never comes. When and
where will be born that last happy generation, who are
to reap all the fruit of these ages of sacrifice ? Will
they wallow in the lost joys of sad women who have
resigned ambitions, and allowed talents to die in this
thankless service ? Will they taste all the experience
that their mothers consented to forego ? Are all these
things stored up for them, like treasure that a miser

will not spend, though he perish in his garret for lack of warmth and nourishment ?

Not so; but rather, for every loss suffered by the fathers, the children will be held debtors.

As regards the fears that are entertained, on all sides, at the prospect of women taking part in political life, or in any occupation which custom has not hitherto recognised as feminine, the advocates of freedom might ask : why nobody has hitherto felt the least alarm about the awful nervous strain which the ideal submissive woman has had to undergo, from time immemorial. Why has nobody considered the danger involved in the bearing and rearing of vast families, and the incessant cares of a household, under conditions, perhaps, of straightened means ? Is there anything in the world that causes more nervous exhaustion than such a combination of duties ? Doctors are, for once, agreed that worry is the most resistless of all taxes upon the constitution. Monotony of life has the same tendency, and a lack of variety in interests and thought undeniably conduces to the lowering of the vitality. Yet nobody has taken fright at the fatal combination of all these nerve-destroying conditions, which belong essentially to the lot of woman under the old *régime*.[1]

The one sort of strain which seems to be feared for the feminine constitution is that of brain-work, although, as a matter of fact, mental effort, if not too prolonged and severe, enhances and does not exhaust the vitality.

It is true, it cannot be carried on simultaneously with great physical exertion. To go on having children, year

---

[1] " The idea of the pilgrimage (to the hill-top) was to get away from the endless and nameless circumstances of every-day existence, which by degrees build a wall about the mind, so that it travels in a constantly narrowing circle. . . . *This is all—there is nothing more;* this is the reiterated preaching of house-life . . . the constant routine of house-life, the same work, the same thought in the work, the little circumstances daily recurring will dull the keenest edge of work."—" The Story of My Heart," by Richard Jefferies.

after year, superintending them and the home while
doing other work outside, would indeed have disastrous
consequences, but who would wish to see women doing
anything so insane ?   Such a domestic treadmill is
stupid and brutal enough, without the addition of
the mental toil.   It is the treadmill that calls for
modification.

If the new movement had no other effect than to
rouse women to rebellion against the madness of large
families, it would confer a priceless benefit on humanity.

We are accustomed to hear a great deal about the
mother's joys, especially from male enthusiasts, on this
ever-popular theme ; but there are, here and there,
evidences of sentiments of another nature on the part
of mothers ; and, significantly enough, in those most
spontaneous expressions of feeling—ancient folk-songs
and lullabies.   The *Athenæum* of August 1895, in
reviewing a collection of lullabies, says of the
authoress :—

"She has chosen very pretty ones, though many of them are not
so much cradle-songs proper . . . as expressions of the mother's
weariness and longing for the moment when the child, which has
been more or less of a burden to her all day, will sleep and let her
rest.

'O haste thee, babe, that so I too
May get at last to sleep,'

says the Italian mother." [1]

These sentiments are not often expressed, but no keen

---

[1] It may be worth while to give the other examples, as they are somewhat striking. The Welsh mother (as the reviewer remarks) is still
more explicit :—

" 'Tis I that nurse the babe, and rock
His cradle to and fro,
'Tis I that lull and lullay him
Unceasingly and low.

" On this day's morn, alack ! he cried
From midnight until three,

M

observer can fail to see that they are very wide-spread, even among the orthodox.

Let any reasonable woman expend the force that, under the old order, would have been given to the production of, say, the third, fourth, or fifth child, upon work of another kind, and let her also take the rest and enjoyment, whatever her work, that every human being needs. It is certain that the one or two children which such a woman might elect to bear, would have cause to be thankful that their mother threw over " the holiest traditions of her sex," and left insane ideas of woman's duties and functions to her grandmothers.

But there are many modern women, who in their own way, are quite as foolish as those grandmothers, for they are guilty of the madness of trying to live the old domestic life without modification, while entering, at the same time, upon a larger field of interests, working simultaneously body and brain under conditions of excitement and worry. This insanity, which one might indeed call by a harsher name, will be punished, as all overstrain is punished. But the cure for these evils is not to immerse women more completely in the cares of domestic life, but to simplify its methods, by the aid of a little intelligence, and by means which there is no

> But it is I that lose my sleep,
> The care is all on me,"

and so on in the same strain ; but her complaint is nothing to that of the Scotch mother, who sings :—

> " Hee O ! wee O !
> What wad I do wi' you ?
> Black is the life
> That I lead wi' you.

> " Ower mony o' you ;
> Little for to gie you ;
> Hee O ! wee O !
> What wad I do wi' you ?" &c.

These verses at least reveal the existence, from very ancient times, of a certain lack of appreciation of " a woman's crowning joy."

space to discuss here. The present waste of energy in
our homes is simply appalling.

Surely the distortion of the faculties of one sex would
be a ruinous price to pay for the physical safety of the
race, even if it secured it, which it does not, but, on the
contrary, places it in peril. If it were really necessary
to sacrifice women for this end, then progress would
be impossible. Society would nourish within itself the
germ of its own destruction. Woman, whose soul had
been (by supposition) sacrificed for the sake of her body,
must for ever constitute an element of reaction and
decay, which no unaided efforts of man could counteract.
The influence, hereditary and personal, which women
possess, secures to them this terrible revenge.

But there is another consideration in connection with
this point, which Mrs Lynn Linton overlooks. If the
woman is to be asked to surrender so much because she
has to produce the succeeding generation, why is the
father left altogether out of count? Does *his* life leave
no mark upon his offspring? Or does Mrs Lynn Linton,
perhaps, think that if the mother takes precautions for
their welfare to the extent of surrendering her whole
existence, the father may be safely left to take no precautions at all?

" The clamour for political rights," this lady says, " is
woman's confession of sexual enmity. Gloss it over as
we may, it comes to this in the end. No woman who
loves her husband would usurp his province." Might
one not retort: No man who loves his wife would seek
to hamper her freedom? But in fact, nothing could be
more false than the assertion that the new ideals imply
sexual enmity. On the contrary, they contemplate a
relationship between the sexes which is more close and
sympathetic than any relationship that the world has
yet seen.

Friendship between husband and wife, on the old terms,
was almost impossible. Where there is power on the

one hand and subordination on the other, whatever the relationship that may arise, it is not likely to be that of friendship.

Separate interests and ambitions, minds moving on different planes—all this tended to make strangers of those who had to pass their lives together, hampered eternally by the false sentiment which made it the right of one to command, and the duty of the other to obey. But now, for the first time in history, we have come within measurable distance of a union between man and woman, as distinguished from a common bondage. Among the latest words that have been said by science, on this subject, are the following from the " Evolution of Sex," by Professors Geddes and Thompson—

> "Admitting the theory of evolution, we are not only compelled to hope, but logically compelled to assume, that those rare fruits of an apparently more than earthly paradise of love, which only the forerunners of the race have been privileged to gather, or, it may be, to see from distant heights, are yet the realities of a daily life to which we and ours may journey."

As for Mrs Lynn Linton's accusations against the " wild women," as regards their lack of principle and even of common honesty, they are surely themselves a little " wild."

The rest of her charges are equally severe, and they induce one to wonder through what unhappy experiences the lady has passed, since she appears never to have encountered a single good or generous woman outside the ranks of her own followers—unless it were a born idiot here and there ! Even the men who disagree with her, are either knaves or fools !

I would exhort the " wild women " to be more tolerant than this, and to admit that they number many able opponents, as well as many wise and generous supporters, among both men and women. The matter is too serious to be wrangled about. The adversaries of the " wild woman " have hit upon not a few truths in

their time, and have done much service in forcing the
opposite party to think their position out, in all its bear-
ings. From the " wild " point of view, of course, the
conclusions of Mrs Lynn Linton and her school seem
false, because they deal with facts, when they find them,
without sufficiently comparing and balancing them with
other facts, perhaps rather less obvious ; and, above all,
without taking into account the one very significant
fact: that the human constitution is as sensitive as a
weather-glass to its conditions, and susceptible of infinite
modification.

Mrs Lynn Linton expresses herself with indignation
against the mothers who allow their daughters to have
a certain amount of freedom ; " they know," she says,
" the dangers of life, and from what girls ought to be
protected. If they disregard the wisdom of experience,
on whose soul lies the sin ? Is the wolf to blame who
passes through the open fence into the fold ? "

Yes, certainly he is ; the negligence of the shepherd
does not turn the wolf into a lamb. But, as a matter
of fact, the illustration is not a true one. The social
" wolf " attacks the lambs only if the lambs exceed the
limits of what society expects of them, as regards liberty.
A girl, walking alone in London, meets with no trouble,
whereas in Paris or Vienna she might run the risk of
annoyance. It is clearly in the interests of every one
that those limits should be, as much as possible, extended.
The greater the number of girls who are allowed this independence, the less the risk, and the less the hindrances
and difficulties for all concerned. The burden on mothers
of a host of daughters who cannot stir from their
homes without a bodyguard, is very severe. Mrs Lynn
Linton does her best to check the tendency to a greater
self-reliance among girls, and would throw society back
upon its path towards its abandoned errors.

The quarrel, in fact, between Mrs Lynn Linton and
her opponents is simply the time-honoured quarrel

between yesterday and to-day, between reaction and progress, between decaying institutions and the stirrings of a new social faith.

There was a time when Mrs Lynn Linton had ardent sympathies with the struggle of a soul towards a new hope, but that is all over; and she has no sympathy left for any belief which is not " hallowed by time;" for any attitude of mind (at least in her own sex) that is not unquestioning and submissive.

The world will occupy itself in this conflict for a long time to come ; and the issue must entangle itself with the great economic problem that this age has to solve, the whole matter of the relation of the sexes being therein involved.

If this generation is wise, it will conduct these two movements in a fashion new to history. Taking warning by the experience of the past, it will avoid the weak old argument of violence, as a strong and intelligent teacher avoids the cowardly and senseless device of corporal punishment. It will conduct its revolution by means of the only weapon that has ever given a victory worth winning—intelligence.

Mankind has tried blood and thunder long enough ; they have not answered. The counter-stroke is as strong as the original impetus, and we expiate our error in the wearisome decades of a reaction. No revolution can be achieved to any purpose, that is not organic; it must rest upon a real change in the sentiment and constitution of humanity. We are not governed by armies and police, we are governed by sentiment ; and this power that lies in human opinion is becoming strengthened with every advance that we make in civilisation, and in the rapidity with which ideas are communicated from man to man, and from nation to nation. The whole course of progress tends towards the dethronement of brute force in favour of the force of thought. Let women lead the way in preferring calm argument to excited vituperation, even when vituperation might be well deserved by its object; let them at least strive to conduct their movement as, on the whole, it may be claimed to have been conducted hitherto, in a steady, philosophic, and genial spirit; regarding the opposition that they receive, as much as possible from the point of view of the student rather than of the partisan, realising that in this greatest of all social revolutions, they must expect the fiercest resistance; that men, in opposing them, are neither better nor worse than all human beings of either sex have shown themselves to be, as soon as they become possessors of power over their fellows. The noblest can scarcely stand the test, and of average men and women it makes bullies and tyrants. If this general fact be borne in mind throughout the struggle, it will be easier to avoid these feelings of bitterness and rancour which the sense of injustice infallibly creates. It will remind those engaged in the encounter to regard it in the historic spirit, while not abating, in the smallest degree, their enthusiasm for the cause of justice and of progress. It will teach them not to be too much dismayed, if the change for which they have striven so hard must be delayed until long after they are dead, and all those who would have rejoiced in it are no longer there to see the sun rise over the promised land. It will teach them, too, to realise more strongly than most of us are inclined to do, that men and women are brothers and sisters, bound to stand or fall together; that in trying to raise the position of women, they are serving at least as much the men who are to be their husbands or sons; that, in short— to quote the saying of Hegel—"The master does not become really free till he has liberated his slave."

PHASES OF HUMAN DEVELOPMENT

PART I

" It is with men as with trees—if you lop off their finest branches, . . . the wounds will be healed over into some rough boss, some rude excrescence, . . . the trivial erring life which we insult with our harsh blame, may be but as the unsteady motion of a man whose best limb is withered."—GEORGE ELIOT.

THE teaching of History defies the popular notion that elemental human passions are entirely beyond the power of circumstance.[1]

Like most popular notions, this one is false and superficial. No instinct, however strong, but has shown itself, in certain conditions, tame and subservient ; no heroism, however great, is beyond the strength of *average* man or woman, when demanded as a duty by the creeds of the race. But to this we must add : no crime, however base, no cruelty, however fiendish, is shrunk from when religious enthusiasm dictates, or when social law commands.[2]

[1] " Tel est l'esprit qui nous gouverne, nous ne pouvons souffrir ce qui s'écarte de nos vues étroites, de nos petites habitudes. De la mesure de nos idées nous faisons la borne de celle des autres. Tout ce qui va au delà nous blesse."—Chateaubriand, " Essai sur les Revolutions."

The notion held by many that the " wisdom of ages " has ordained our institutions can scarcely survive historical research, for this generally reveals them as monuments of centuries of accumulated folly, which can hardly claim admiration from the fact that they have escaped deserved attack for so long.

[2] The records of many religions prove that even the instinct of self-preservation can be overborne without difficulty. Instances of astonishing heroism, demanded as an ordinary custom, will occur to every one, as existing among savage tribes. Examples of cruelty are still more numerous. Putting aside the more terrible cases, it is strange to read accounts of hunting expeditions among (for example) the North American Indians, which make one realise how very close to the aboriginal state our own sportsmen still are. The savage's skilful method of killing and of snaring the game would kindle enthusiasm in the hearts of men and

It must be understood that man, in any age and country, is liable to revert to a state of savagery, if conditions favour such a retrogression. His surroundings gradually persuade him into harmony with themselves, not only by direct action upon his own nature, but by exterminating those of his contemporaries who are unable to endure them. The race, therefore, even more than the individual, is clay in the hands of the potter: Circumstance.

Extremes of good and evil may be found side by side, even in the same person, if one part of his nature has been cultivated, while the other has been left unaltered. Thus we find men who might justly be called good, committing deeds that are actually atrocious, simply because, in certain directions, their instincts have not been redeemed from the primitive state. There are plenty of very good men—as we half-civilised beings esteem goodness—who are simply and obviously savage as regards their treatment of animals, inflicting upon them, for the sake of what is called " sport," or " science," protracted tortures perhaps, without a qualm or a suspicion of offence. In modern life, we see a sort of dual conscience; fairly active as regards human beings, but scarcely awake at all in respect to other races of suffering creatures. It is not the capability for pain or pleasure in others which arouses man's sense of responsibility, but the fact of belonging to his own division of creation. It is not moral development, but tradition

brothers who call themselves civilised. These same American tribes, who during peace seem to show many good and even kindly qualities, become in time of war nothing less than demons. The description of the tortures that they love to inflict upon their enemies—trying always to take them alive in order to enjoy that pleasure—are too terrible for the imagination to endure. When the victorious band returns home, after the wailing for the fallen has ceased, wild war-whoops are set up to announce the number of captives. And then the whole settlement turns out, and the prisoners are led through two rows of women and children, who are eager to commence the horrible ceremony of torture and execution.

that decides his conduct. Clearly, therefore, exemplary characters afford no presumption whatever that the institutions which they support are worthy of respect. But while there is nothing so atrocious in itself that habit will not reconcile, and even endear to human beings of excellent disposition, they will not commit an atrocity that belongs to a past epoch. Only those who fall below the average will revert to forms of savagery that are disallowed by their century. To this fact we owe our progress. The conduct of the ordinary man fluctuates around the accepted standard as a centre, and thus we slowly make way by a successive raising of the standard. Such conduct, revolving round its habitual centre, is drawn upwards in a continuous spiral, without any increase of effort on the part of the individual towards higher conceptions of right and wrong.

On either side of the average man, who constitutes the immediate ruling force of society, we have those below and those above the average. From the one class we get our criminals; from the other, the makers of new standards. Our aim, then, must obviously be to raise the standards, and therefore the average man, until these have succeeded in holding in thrall, and finally extirpating the original savage, who still utters his disturbing war-whoop in the heart of our most respectable citizens. We must seek to play upon the more human elements, so that the desires become, on the whole, more fruitful in happiness of the lasting and true sort than are the desires of the half-developed being who now, *faute de mieux*, is known as civilised man.

It is all a matter of conditions. The fatal and common mistake is to take humanity as we happen to find it in our age and country, and fit our measures to its evil and its ignorance. We must on no account admit that local " human nature " as a constant factor, but must regard it as a mere register of the forces that chance to be at work at the moment, and of the forces that have been at work in the past.

Different centuries produce different types of humanity, though born of the same race. The best of men will commit deeds in one era at which the worst would hesitate in another. The standard, therefore, as we have seen, is all-important in determining morality, and not less so than is the supply of air and food and water in regulating the public health. Standards, be it observed, may vary from the sublime to the ridiculous.

Italy, during the times of the Middle Ages and the Renaissance, affords an interesting example of their influence. Without a central authority to hold the nobles in check, the country became a prey to the powerful families, whose perpetual struggles, between themselves, and with the Republics, show clearly the result of arbitrary power upon the nature of man. It is certainly not probable that Italy, during this period, produced a sudden increase of abnormally evil-minded men, foredoomed to crime from their birth. The worst of the Borgias and the Visconti were merely the product of their age, which encouraged crime, and rewarded the finer qualities with contempt. The story of the little son of the chief Minister of the Duke of Athens, who, during the latter's rule in Florence, used to delight in being present at the tortures ordered by his father, is a striking example of the effect of circumstance upon character. The child had acquired a taste for these scenes, and used to plead that the tortures might be prolonged beyond the time appointed, asking for special kinds to be inflicted, because he enjoyed witnessing the extreme agony that they caused.[1] This seems diabolical to the modern conscience. Yet in all probability there is not a sweet and innocent child in a British nursery, at this moment, who might not, under certain conditions, have

[1] " Histoire des Républiques Italiennes du Moyen Age."—Sismondi.

developed the same ferocity as that which horrifies us
in the little savage of the Middle Ages. The cruelty of
boys is proverbial. Training checks them at a certain
point, but not the sense of pity. The savage is overcome in man exactly so far as his tradition takes him,
but not an inch farther. At that tide-line his mercy
abruptly stops. Woe to those whom he encounters on
the wrong side of it !

During the period of the Renaissance, the possession
of power seems to have induced, in most of the seigneurs
of Italy, a sort of insanity of cruelty, such as we find
among the Roman Emperors, after their rule became
absolute. When there is no criterion but a man's own
conscience, even if that conscience be originally of
exceptional vigour, he ends by losing all balance in
his ideas of right and wrong: he becomes morally
dizzy or insane. Among the Italian tyrants, this
" blood-madness," as it was named, recalls the conduct of the savages who torture their prisoners to
death — as, for instance, when one of the Visconti
ordered that a captive foe should have the agony of
his punishment protracted during forty-eight hours,
or when the seigneur, in a fit of anger, thrust an
offending servant on to the fire, and held him there
until he died. It would be inexcusable to bring forward these painful instances, were it not that these
facts in human nature are generally either ignored, or
attributed to wrong causes.

Such facts *have* to be kept in mind, for they warn us
how alarmingly dependent we all are for our peace and
safety, on the conditions that are everywhere busy around
us, forming the sentiments of average humanity ; that
average which is becoming more and more the real
potentate in the democracy.

Past events may serve as warnings ; for wherever
arbitrary power has existed, there, in exact correspon-
dence with the degree of the power, tyranny, and suffering

have sprung up as a result. From the Emperor of all the Russias to the irascible father of a family, who makes his subordinates tremble at his voice, cause and effect are identical. Moreover, another law is equally well established: That the victim of tyranny will always tyrannise mercilessly when *his* chance comes. He has seldom seen any other use made of authority, and not being inventive, he does not presume to strike out a new line for himself. He would probably not find his fellow creatures encouraging, if he did so.

Remembering that most people imitate, but do not evolve, we need not feel surprised that this should be the fact. It may be laid down as a maxim that ordinary men and women will always oppress their neighbours exactly as severely as their neighbours will allow themselves to be oppressed. Conscience is no check, for its possessors will force others to act upon the conclusions of that conscience, and feel rather a glow of self-satisfaction than any suspicion that they are committing an act of violent oppression, in so doing.

In the domain of the conscience, above all others, a man demands to be free ; yet it is in that domain especially that others seem to feel themselves most justified in coercing him.

Now it is obvious that just such conditions of power, on the one hand, and subjection on the other, have been busy for centuries in the very heart and centre of our existence. We must not be deluded into the belief that any of the relationships of life, however close, form a safeguard against that abuse of power. As a matter of fact, it is generally the nearest and dearest over whom the most rigid tyranny is exercised ; for here the opportunities are greater, the excuses more numerous, and for some mysterious reason, the desire of rule more eager than in any other case. The amount of interference and of uninvited criticism that people accept from even their distant relations would never be offered or endured on any other plea.

Here and there, indeed, we come upon exceptional natures to whom these remarks do not apply. In the annals of crime, even in the worst epochs, some finer, more pitiful character shines out to redeem his age; honourable in the midst of treachery, merciful and tolerant when his contemporaries seemed unable to conduct their affairs without the help of the thumb-screw and the rack.[1] Such natures, happily for us all, have appeared in every era, at rare intervals, but it is not by any means inconceivable that the conditions of life, already unfavourable to their development, should become so hopelessly untoward, that they would grow rarer and rarer, and finally, perhaps, die out altogether. In other words, society might become incapable of pro-ducing the finer types of mankind, and might gradually sink in its standards till it destroyed itself. Such may almost be said to have been the fate of some of the stagnating Eastern nations.[2]

Society, as a whole, does not conduct itself on any reasoned scheme, but works very much after the fashion of a hive of bees, who, with all their apparent intelli-gence, are blind victims of some inborn force, and differ from human beings in never developing a variation of the type distinct enough to modify their organisation. Perhaps their lack of the recording faculty deprives their

---

[1] "He only knows how to conquer who knows how to forgive," was a saying of Lorenzo di Medici, a maxim which he adhered to even in the case of treacherous attempts upon his life.—See Roscoe's "Life of Lorenzo di Medici."

[2] ". . . toutes les fois qu'un peuple placé en tête de l'humanite est devenu stationnaire, les germes du progrès qui se trouvaient dans son sein, ont été aussitôt transportés ailleurs, sur un sol où ils pouvaient se développer : et l'on a vu constamment dans ce cas, le peuple, rebelle à la loi humaine, s'abîmer et s'anéantir comme écrasé sous le poids d'un anathème."—Bazard et Enfantin, disciples of St Simon.   See also "Emancipation of the Family," page 23.

variations of influence, so that apparently their habits never alter. The same tendency is to be noticed in certain human races, (as, for example, the Chinese); and this must be because there is also something in *their* social form that renders nugatory the existence of those individuals who differ from the average.

Now it is clear that (among other probable causes) the subject condition of women must act as a predisposing influence in this direction, by rendering more infrequent the birth of these exceptional types. Varieties are obviously unlikely to occur often in a race, when half its numbers are placed in similar conditions, trained in the same fashion, excellent though it may be, and when precisely the same set of qualities and instincts— to the discouragement of others—are called forth, age after age, and exaggerated, as far as possible, in every individal of that vast multitude.[1]   Chances of variation, in such circumstances, must evidently be few. Moreover, the unusual natures, when they *did* appear, would be likely to be destroyed or neutralised. In short, the subjection of women, whether it be complete and logical, as in the East, or modified and irrational, as among ourselves, is like a vast machine carefully constructed to stamp out and mangle smooth all varieties and all superiorities in the race. Among nations where the influences to which women are exposed are most completely uniform, there we find the fewest men of remarkable character, the least movement, the least vitality, the least liberty, even among the governing sex, and the most wretched social condition generally. It obviously *must* be so. Yet these are the conditions that so many people still cling to with perverse affection, mistaking for a safeguard that which is, in truth, the element of danger in every civilisation.

If it be acknowledged, in theory, that man is the product of his surroundings, it is ignored in practice.

[1] See note, p. 175.

We shake our heads over " human nature," or we pin our faith to its inherent goodness, not seeing that such optimism and pessimism are dependent rather on the state of the liver than on that of the judgment. Man is neither an angel gone astray nor a devil struggling to reform ; he is the result of his past—and its accuser.

It is not, indeed, that conditions are all in the formation of character, and original nature nothing. That is a theory which common experience disproves. But their power in calling forth, or leaving dormant, as the case may be, the various qualities of that original nature —itself *au fond* the handiwork of past conditions— has surely never yet been fully comprehended. What we call character depends upon the balance of certain forces, and their proportionate influence on the thoughts and actions. A large family of children brought up under one roof, are often strikingly unlike, although the influences have been the same in every case. But who can doubt that if those influences had been radically different, each one of those children would have grown up with characteristics other than those which he now possesses ? Is it possible to suppose that an obstinate child would turn out precisely the same under the care of a wise and sympathetic mother, as he would become in the hands of one who was bad-tempered and stupid ?

It is the chemical union of native bias with daily circumstance which has for product a human character. The same processes are going on in the race on a larger scale : the characteristics of class, of profession, of sex, forming, for good or ill, in strict harmony with the predominating forces. The reign of law is as absolute here as in the case of a falling stone or a discharge of electricity. Many of the social problems that seem so insoluble thus appear simple. The cause of our woes becomes obvious, and we can observe the storing-up of woes for our successors, through our present sins and follies.

Now, a doctor who has made a sound diagnosis, has, at least, taken the first necessary step towards curing his patient. The most brilliant treatment for apoplexy might prove murderous if applied to a case of measles. Thence we see the supreme importance of a correct diagnosis of the social ailments.

To any one who thoroughly realises all this and its far-reaching consequences, the study of history gathers an extraordinary interest, though often a somewhat painful one. If the human race may be likened to the obstinate child, his past has certainly been to him an ill-tempered and a stupid mother !

In Sismondi's account of the defence of Cesena by Marzia, wife of the seigneur of Forli—who was himself engaged at the moment in withstanding the siege of that town—we find a striking example of the action of surroundings in moulding character, where the original forces were evidently very strong. It also gives a general idea of the sentiment of that age regarding the duties of women. The influence of their position upon the nature of the race, with its effects, direct and indirect, would afford a subject for a new science.

With a young son and daughter, and a counsellor of her husband's choosing, Marzia shut herself up in Cesena, prepared to hold out against the Papal forces to the last extremity. The people soon surrendered the lower part of the town, and Marzia retired to the citadel with a few followers. Finding that the counsellor was in secret treaty with the enemy, she promptly had his head cut off on the walls of the fortress, taking upon herself the duties of governor and captain. "She never after that took off her cuirass, and the enemies saw her perpetually at the head of her soldiers." The besiegers were throwing huge blocks at the citadel, and they were busy undermining the walls, so that the situation became desperate. At this juncture, Marzia's father appeared with a message from the Legate : that the latter would offer her honourable terms if she would surrender the town. The old man used every entreaty to induce his daughter to avoid the last horrors of a siege. Marzia's reply is characteristic: " My father, when you gave me to my lord, you commanded me above all things to obey him always ; that I have done up to to-day, that will I do unto death. He confided to my care this fortress, and forbade me to abandon it for any reason whatsoever, without having received fresh orders from him. That is my duty ; what is death or danger to me ? I obey, and I judge not."

Here we see the strange effect upon a resolute character of the traditions of the time. Marzia does not disdain to speak of herself as being " given " to her " lord ; " she who is seemingly almost without fear, " obeys," but " judges not." Her father was unable to persuade her to alter her resolution. She held out until the soldiers refused to remain to be buried in a town which was now perilously suspended over the excavations of the besiegers. The Legate assigned her a ship in the harbour of Ancona for her prison. With such steadfastness, great things might have been accomplished ; but this singular woman threw all the force of her character into a sort of arrogant meekness. Throughout her life, she had been suppressing her own powers by her own will-force, cultivating a spirit of blind obedience, while encouraging in her lord that tendency to abuse unquestioned authority, which the merit of the angel Gabriel himself would scarcely be proof against, under temptations so importunate.

What conditions have been at work in determining the qualities of women, and in what manner have their qualities, so acquired, reacted upon the state of society generally, upon the nature of men, and upon the morality of the race ?

Let us suppose that we had to explain, as clearly as possible, the dominant facts of our social history to some visitant from another planet. In order to make our present order even intelligible to such a mind, it would be necessary to point out that it consisted in a vast agglomeration of remnants of other and earlier systems —a sort of pudding-stone of spiritual geology. Among us —we should explain when questioned as to our educational modes—the fate of each human being was arbitrarily determined at birth. Their sex, and that alone, decided us to educate our girls in a certain restrictive fashion, irrespective of every other fact. Their sex, on the other hand, decided us to educate our boys with the view of developing whatever talent they might possess.

The unbiassed intelligence might here object, that it would be just as reasonable to classify our population according to the colour of their eyes or the shape of their noses, and might point out that if such a division *had* been made (the possession of blue eyes assuring one a liberal education and comparative freedom), there would undoubtedly have grown up a firm belief that Heaven had bestowed certain eternal characteristics on that blue-eyed race, while it had ordained for the less fortunate owners of brown or hazel orbs, lesser ability and an inferior position.

The great difference in training would, in a generation or two, create certain *real* differences between the two groups (even in the absence of any unlikeness of physical constitution to accelerate the divergence). And thus the prejudice, in course of time, would receive apparent justification. Yet on equally good evidence, might one argue that the nature (for example) of lawyers was eternally and by natural ordinance, different from that of doctors and clergymen. The daily conditions of life create habits, needs, temptations ; they assail their victim with inces-

sant urgings in certain directions, with incessant arguments that appeal to one side or other of his original
character. They lull to rest other impulses that might
have been vigorous; they thrust and lure and soothe and
manipulate, till the man becomes their own, not of necessity their slave, but none the less their handiwork.

We should only laugh at any one who urged that,
for instance, a sailor had been from birth incapable of
understanding a legal document; that had he chosen the
barrister's profession, instead of his own, he would, to the
end of his days, have betrayed an ineradicable tendency
to run up masts and dance the hornpipe. There are
indeed cases of very marked bias which nothing can
overcome entirely, but these are rare. Even upon these,
moreover, the power of the magician: Circumstance, is
exercised in subtle methods and devices.

Now, it is popularly understood that the whole race
of women has been specially created in order to occupy
precisely the position which they occupy at this era, with
precisely the amount of freedom now accorded, neither
more nor less—for the happy moment has apparently
arrived when matters have reached perfection. And
that precise position, we are also given to understand,
is indicated by the qualities and instincts that women
manifest or are said to manifest. If we are to believe
this, we must also conclude that Nature, in her wisdom,
intended soldiers to hold themselves rigidly erect;
doctors to possess a peculiar gait as of intending crime;
ballet-dancers to stand for hours comfortably on one toe,
and that they were all born with those achievements in
view. Truly the age of superstition has not yet passed
away!

It is not usually denied that women have, as a rule,
small opportunity for intellectual progress; but nobody
seems to doubt that the best conditions for their moral
career are assured. But this, too, is open to dispute.

To be forced, by popular clamour, into a blind self-anni-
hilation, is not really conducive to the health of the moral
faculties; and this is why the goodness of so many
women has in it a morbid quality. Von Hartmann says:
"Nothing can be reasonably designated moral except a will
self-determining and legislating for itself." The ordinary
training of a woman does not make clear the rights of
other classes and kinds of beings, It does nothing but
enjoin a narrow duty; obedience to the demands of immediate conditions, and reverence only for those ties that
are fortuitous, or that are sanctified by legal forms. Not
tenderness and sympathy for all that lives and can suffer
is the underlying idea of feminine goodness, but devotion
to individuals who are selected by mere accident of birth
or hazard of circumstance. And this merely instinctive
form of attachment is applauded as a woman's highest
impulse and privilege.

Nor is she more reasonably or justly treated in regard
to the choice of her avocations. If a girl shows a tendency to any consecutive work of an unorthodox kind, she
is looked at with disfavour, and more than half her energies
are consumed in struggling against the innumerable petty
obstacles that are placed in her way. Still more is her
power sapped by the deadly atmosphere of discouragement which benumbs both hope and initiative. Who
can tell how much serviceable talent is not thus turned
into morbid developments, physical and mental? Extraordinary and insidious difficulties have to be contended
with, on all hands. The woman's confidence in herself
is starved or shaken. Instead of working on without
question at the instigation of her talent, she stops to
wonder morbidly if indeed she has the gift or the justification. Her training tends always to make her readily
accept moral censure. Repeatedly assured that she is
selfish and wrong-headed, the struggler loses heart, and
in most cases can be finally talked into the belief that
it is her true duty to make antimacassars, or that she

lives the higher life by playing dominoes with her maiden aunt. By this means, the community is deprived of the result of work performed with the efficiency that is assured by a natural bent. It is further impoverished by the loss of the fruits of the strengthened character that follows any end faithfully pursued; an effect which carries invigorating counsels far and wide, just as the influences disintegrate and slacken of those who allow themselves to drift through life with the prevailing current.

This process of suppressing the variant types among women has been going on amongst us age after age, the suppression being only less complete now than it was in the darkest of the Dark Ages. There were always plenty of maiden aunts to play dominoes with, and generation after generation grew up with the same old traditions and views of life; girls who did not marry and produce daughters to entertain the maiden aunts, themselves becoming maiden aunts to be entertained.

Nor does the married woman fare better. If, after keeping the house, with its minute and multitudinous demands and interruptions, bearing and training children, and performing all her duties to her relations and friends to their entire satisfaction, a woman finds that she has strength and courage for any work of her own, then she may, without serious offence, so employ the odds and ends of her energy and time. But even then, she runs the risk—nay, incurs the certainty—of being dubbed selfish. Woe to her if the force within her is strong enough to make its imprisonment painful ! Woe to her sisters if the immemorial maxims preserved in lavender, generation after generation, for the instruction of her sex, induce her to renounce the essential side of her nature, in order to win the applause of the orthodox, or, to put it more accurately, to avoid their censure ! For every such submission adds to the strength of the tyranny from which she suffers, and increases the burden for her successors. Renunciation thus often becomes a form of luxury. To a woman, self-sacrifice is generally the path of least resistance. It is doubtless much easier to submit and be " unselfish." Mephistopheles, in Clough's poem, is always whispering humble counsels. To cultivate a sense of virtue, which renunciation, however blind and stupid, is always warranted to produce, demands far less courage than to stand out against aggression, and submit to be classed with the unregenerate. Yet this is often the real duty of those who desire to aid in the progress of their generation.

It is true that under present conditions complete resistance to aggression is not really possible to a woman. There are methods of compulsion which scarcely admit of defiance. She can be placed, if her resistance grows desperate, between the devil and the deep sea : between the alternatives of submission in marriage to whatever may be required of her,—injuries and insults if need be,—or the surrender of her children, perhaps into hands that she regards, as of all others, the most unfit to train them. This is the weapon by which many a wife has been forced to obedience, as by the application of the thumbscrew. The feeling that was aroused in the public mind by the character of Ibsen's " Nora," shows what a mother would have to contend with, in popular sentiment, who dared the terrors of the social torture-chamber, and thus threatened the efficacy of this venerable instrument of government.

Such, then, are, roughly speaking, the conditions to which one-half of the race have been subjected during the most favourable epochs of their history. Their fate, in earlier times was, of course, more obviously tragic, for then manners and morals were more brutal.[1]

Now, we have already seen that the health of society depends upon its power of producing variations in the type ; the decline of certain races being the result of a

[1] See " The Lot of Woman under the Rule of Man," p. 92.

failure of this faculty, or the fruits of an organisation which suppresses their development and influence. For that reason, then, if for no other, the conditions of life for women have been a national disaster; for no race can afford to risk the results of such paralysing uniformity. We may rest assured that our downfall will, sooner or later, be the penalty of folly so obstinate and so gigantic.

PART II

" We transmit, must transmit, being mothers,
What we are to mankind."
—CHARLOTTE STETSON.

Two great dangers to the race are involved in the bondage imposed upon women. The suppression of "sports"
or varieties has been already treated. We now come to
the injury.entailed upon men, as the sons, husbands, and
brothers of bondswomen.

A man has been brought up, from earliest childhood,
to regard a woman as of less importance than himself :
he sees her trained to minister to his comfort, and to
make herself pleasing in his eyes. He finds the respectable British matron eager to see her daughters marry
well :—does she not know, poor woman, that if they do
not marry well, society offers them small chance of doing
well in any other way ? Among the classes for whom
the man of the world would feel called upon to profess
respect, the voices of duty and religion mingle with that
of self-interest, in counselling submission ; while in the
class that he would openly despise, the necessity to earn
a living, and the dread of slaving at starvation wages,
provides a motive for the bargain which, according to
popular incoherence, disgraces beyond redemption one of
the parties to it, while it leaves the other a pillar of
society. Is any one so optimistic as to believe that
from conditions such as these, it is possible to produce
a community wherein all the worst instincts of mankind
shall not run wild ?

If it be true that character is the product of native

impulse in combination with daily circumstance,[1] what is the character that might be expected in the average man ? Is he not almost foredoomed to corruption ? What chance has he of escaping unharmed from such a conspiracy of destiny ? Had it been the object of some untoward spirit to create a corrupt and desperate community, how could that evil genius have done it better than by placing one sex at the mercy of the other, and teaching both to regard the arrangement as ordained by God and sanctioned by man ? Leaving the doctrine to do its work, we should find it capable, in a few years, of ruining the character of a company of saints, much more that of a race of ordinary sinners.

This *must* be so, even if influences were otherwise favourable. But so far from this, our social influences all conspire to the same disaster. In the struggle for a livelihood, existence for the majority is lacking in savour, unredeemed by that interest in the mere pageant of life which may bring moments of happiness even in the hardest lot.

" It is not too bold a thing to say that the mind of man once cultivated, he will see around him the Paradise that he laments he has lost. For one Paradise lost, he will sing a thousand that he has gained."

Without internal resources to brighten the dull ways of daily toil, the imperfectly developed human being, subject to all the burdens of civilisation without enjoying its highest gifts, is liable to find only pleasures of the grosser sort attractive. He is thrown upon the mercy of the mere savage within him, whose appetites nothing in his home training, or in the philosophy of the world, seriously teaches him to control.

Thus the plot thickens, and the hero of the drama of life finds himself attacked from every side. If he escape one foe, he is liable to fall into the power of another.

[1] See preceding article.

There is so little to help him. Not only is the whole scheme of life inimical, but all its details bring contributions to his downfall. His nerves, and therefore his self-control and will-force, have been more or less weakened by the exciting pressure of modern life, and his whole nature rendered by so much the less fresh and sound in its instincts. Granting all the advantages to be obtained from public school life, can it be considered as a good preparation for the battle of existence, and the difficulties that are to follow?

The mere minor customs of the time tend in the same direction; the perpetual stimulus of alcohol, "moderate" in quantity though it be, causing at least a harassment to the system, and working in concert with the thousand circumstances of modern life that tend towards overexcitement and exhaustion. Boys, in their school-days, begin to levy this lifelong tax; tobacco soon demands its milder tribute; each payment being, perhaps, small in itself, but all helping to swell that big debt which the average man sets to work to incur, as soon as he has liberty to continue, on his own account and on a grander scale, the errors of his early training. Under this burden, which increases as a river swells with the tributes of tiny streams, he generally finds himself, in middle life, a debtor, without hope of clearing himself of his liabilities. Morally, he also suffers, for worn-out nerves are poor servants to the will and the conscience. Moreover, the will has been weakened by incessant yielding to the desire of the moment.

In his earlier years, he has enjoyed but few chances of companionship with girls whom he respects, because society discourages that good comradeship which is so essential to the development of a healthy feeling. Thence a false sentiment springs up, and men and women tend to forget that it is their common humanity, above all and first of all, that forms the ground of mutual interest, the accident of sex being at present allowed undue weight, and dragged out of all proportion to the facts of existence. In consequence of this state of feeling, and the customs that it engenders, the young man is too often deprived of the help and safety which the friendship of women might have given him in time of need.

Look where he will, there are temptations and snares to his better self. Heredity is his enemy; for have not these very same forces been at work upon the temperament of his ancestors, weakening his own defences, exasperating his primitive " nature " ?

Man, the creature of his conditions, out of which he is fashioned and compounded, body and soul, has small hope indeed of resisting the influences at work upon his character, from the cradle to the grave. Liberty being denied to a whole sex, what can be expected from the other but license ? It is partly because the overwhelming difficulties of the situation are recognised, that little else *is* expected of them. The marvel only is that society has survived at all on such a system. To place the sexes in the relation of possessor and possessed, patron and dependent, is almost equivalent to saying in so many words, to the male half of humanity : " Here is your legitimate prey, pursue it." The existence of the Game Laws regulates, but does not alter, the ultimate relations of sportsmen and their quarry ; neither do the laws of marriage change the fundamental facts in the relations of man to woman. They only render legal and respectable that in them which is most savage.

The freedom, or rather the license, that has been accorded to men, to their own detriment, has obviously been obtained by encroaching on the liberties of women. What has been called liberty was, in fact, broadly speaking, impunity in aggression. The dual standard of morality proves this beyond question. Our laws at present express the sentiment of a society that loves to see its women helpless and imprisoned.

When a small minority have embraced new views on this question, their position is one of peculiar difficulty, for their right and wrong are no longer the right and wrong of their contemporaries.

While they continue to obey the popular view of duty, they are offending their own conscience, and this is, in its very nature, a tragic situation. But as soon as they attempt to act upon their convictions, they are met with outcries on all hands, not merely from the world in general, but from their nearest and dearest.

Suppose, for instance, a woman holds that marriage ought not to confer proprietary rights on either of the partners. This seems to her husband a shocking and intolerable idea. He has married in the ordinary fashion, taking everything for granted as right and fitting, and the current standards as binding on both himself and his wife. He married with certain definite expectations, intending to fulfil what the same authority appointed as *his* duty, and he not unnaturally considers himself ill-used if these expectations are disappointed.

But what can be said of the institution which allows him to possess powers so tremendous over another human being? If a man were living in a community according to whose laws he was the owner of slaves—his whole stake in life depending on them—it would be very hard on him, no doubt, if those slaves were to mutiny, and he were to be left penniless. Why should he, who was at least no worse than others, be thus picked out for affliction? He is honestly desirous of doing his duty by his slaves, as he conceives it, and he cannot understand why they insist on shirking their part of the arrangement. Yet one could scarcely inculcate it as a duty on the part of the slaves to remain in bondage, in order to fulfil the expectations which his country had raised.

Nor can we, with any more fairness, preach to wives to fulfil all the expectations which our marriage laws and customs hold out to the husband. We must remember that as the livelihood of women depends mainly on marriage, the majority have very little more choice as to their status in life than the slave has, who was born of slave parents. Even when the marriage is one of inclination,[1] the

[1] The actual predicament of women in many Roman Catholic countries may be taken, roughly speaking, as a type of their position in relation to society as a whole. The real compulsion that underlies ostensible freedom of choice as regards entering either a cloister or a " sphere " are of about equal cogency.

The position of women in Italy is an interesting study from this point of view.

" The feeling," says Seymour in his " Pilgrimage to Rome," " that the life of the cloister is the only safe and secure protection for an unmarried female, is carefully fostered by the parents, in order to induce their daughters to remain in the cloister. It is no less carefully cherished and fostered by the priesthood, to conceal the penetralia of conventual life ; and so far is this carried, that if a novice, having taken the white veil, should, at the conclusion of her noviciate, refuse to take the black veil, she would be regarded as a reckless and wilful girl, who preferred a life of exposure to the worst temptations in the world, to a life of holiness and peace in a nunnery. Her parents and relations would refuse to receive her ; or, if they did receive her, it would be as a fallen and unhappy one. . . . She would be kept from contact with her other sisters ; she would be removed out of sight, that no stranger should see her ; her name would never be heard in conversation. . . . With such a prospect before her, as a matter of certainty, it ceases to be any cause for astonishment, that the young novice should persevere, and lay aside the white veil, and assume the black, becoming a recluse for life. . . . The daughter is as much regarded as provided for in life in the cloister, as is a daughter in England when settled suitably in marriage, or a son in a preferment ; and therefore we can well conceive the difficulties opposed by parents against all recessions from such engagements.

All this supposes that the young female is free—that she has the opportunity or power to withdraw. And therefore all this applies only or chiefly to the novice, to whom the opportunity is nominally offered, of withdrawing if she wishes. The truth is, that she dare not accept this nominal offer, however much and anxiously she may wish it. The feelings of her own family, and the state of public feeling, impose an insuperable obstacle to her fulfilling her desires, and she passively resigns herself to her hard fate. It is not that she finds her noviciate a happy springtime, as some have imagined ; nor is it that the other nuns, . . . naturally anxious for some new companion to lighten the dull monotony of the cloister, weave all their arts to fascinate and ensnare the novice—it

o

terms which bind the couple are compulsory; and such a marriage—under our present conditions—is *analogous to* (not identical with) a state of slavery willingly incurred for the sake of obtaining some greatly desired good, or of averting some dreaded evil. Yet the slavery remains slavery, however gladly it may be accepted.

It is, moreover, generally accepted in ignorance. It is only day by day, and year by year, that the full significance of the so-called contract becomes revealed to the woman, who has been carefully brought up, without any knowledge of the world—or at any rate, without mental training which would enable her to draw a just conclusion from what she sees.

Is it fair or even sane to demand that the so-called obligations of marriage shall be rigidly fulfilled in such circumstances? Honour does not require the fulfilment of engagements unless they are entered into with complete knowledge, and without any sort of coercion, direct or indirect, or any penalty for refusal. Honour however *does* demand that we shall not take advantage of the assistance of popular opinion to enforce that which has not been agreed to under free conditions—and to which consent ought therefore not to have been asked.

It has been urged even by those who admit that this bondage creates a low moral standard, that the removal of such bondage would be followed by a standard still lower. If this be the case, how is it that we come to be writhing on the horns of this very awkward dilemma? As

is not this that impels and precipitates the fatal step, but it is the impossibility of overcoming the obstacles arising from the feelings of her family and the tone of public feeling on the subject."

And in exactly the same manner, is the young woman in Protestant lands nominally free to refuse marriage and virtually compelled to accept it on almost any terms. Otherwise, penalties of all kinds await her, in consequence of the general organisation of society in relation to her sex, and by reason of the " tone of public feeling on the subject."

these articles have pointed out, we have to thank for this predicament the Uneliminated Savage in our constitution, who scares us from the next important step of progress, preventing us from honouring the relation of man to woman, as we believe, in our hearts, it ought to be honoured.

We consent to degrade that relationship, lest it should be delivered over to our tyrants, to be degraded still more terribly.

There is indeed a pathetic attempt to deny that these compulsory relations *are* debasing, and to act on the good old theory that the Sabbath was not made for man, but man for the Sabbath. But even the staunchest supporters of our present system must see, that if the savage element be not held in check, by some means, both the evil and the difficulty of cure must go on increasing. After a certain time, the strength and life of the people must become exhausted, and then we shall be threatened with the fate that has overtaken so many nations after a certain stage has been reached,—decadence through corruption, or through failure to produce varieties of type.

It is, in fact, inconceivable that a people can go on progressing while they continue to cripple half their numbers. A bird cannot fly long with a broken wing. It is significant that the flight of the creature so injured is not only halting, but it tends to return upon itself, to describe a painful circle, never making way, in spite of all its breathless exertions. The often cited fate of brilliant and apparently sound civilisations, suggests significant reflections with this fact in view.

Society still struggles on, with its broken wing. On no account would it allow the wound to be healed, and if it be suggested that a steadier flight could be achieved by binding up the maimed member, our guides, philosophers, and friends point to the spasmodic movements as a proof of the bird's hopeless inability to move straight.

We must not heal the injury, because it has damaged the constitution of the creature to such an extent that a cure would create the utmost peril to the system. The cripple must be left to pursue its painful way until it sinks, from sheer exhaustion. This in fact is the orthodox typical method of meeting all proposals for reform; and it has pursued us from ages beyond the reach of history. It is an argument which is often reinforced by another argument against the claims of women, which is still more remarkable. Its authors earnestly recommend desistance from all efforts in the direction of freedom, on the ground that so much improvement has been made as regards the position of women during the last twenty or thirty years. Mrs Cady Stanton, who had evidently been much pestered with this baffling form of objection, gives an admirable illustration of its character. "They tell us sometimes," she says, "that if we had only kept quiet, all these desirable things would have come about of themselves. I am reminded of the Greek clown who, having seen an archer bring down a flying bird, remarked sagely, 'You might have saved your arrow, the bird would anyway have been killed by the fall!'"

PART III

THE TYRANNY OF INSTINCT

" But the eternal world
Contains at once the evil and the cure."
—SHELLEY.

IN the movements of modern life, the supremely momentous question is : whether we are to yield to the animal or to the human in our composition. That is to say :—are we to consult what we are pleased to term the natural constitution, or are we rather to take counsel of that element within us, which even now desires an existence impossible to us, only because men have made it so ?

If the body were a rigid affair of mechanism, whose habits and needs were absolutely unmodifiable, so that, in hearkening to the human demands of our being, it were necessary to sacrifice the physical welfare, the race would, indeed, have but little to hope for. But this is far from being the case. The body can create for itself good habits and bad habits ; needs which are purely artificial, yet as peremptory as the demand for food and air. It can, moreover, encourage a natural impulse to such an extent as to make its perpetual gratification a morbid necessity. On the other hand, it can emancipate itself from these claims—a process which, in the course of generations, might be carried to a far greater length than can be hoped for in one lifetime. The more common tendency, however, is to create needs, not to overcome them ; and upon these created needs to found customs and establish conclusions.

The body can be brought into such a state by (for instance) immoderate habits of drinking, that to cease the indulgence would cause great suffering, while to continue it means ruin to the health.   Drunkards and the various victims of narcotics are extreme cases of such a creation of artificial requirements.   When the case *is* an extreme one of this nature, and the indulgence is not a universal habit, but an occasional vice, nobody disputes that the demands thus engendered are unreal, or, rather, that real as they are to the sufferer, they are induced by his own weakness, and do not constitute a primary condition of the race.   The needs of the drunkard and the victim of chloral are not taken into account in social arrangements.

But, let the habit be one in common practice, one that almost every man regards as indispensable.   In *that* case it must be treated seriously, as one of the final conditions of existence ; although it may not be possible to deny that it plays havoc with the welfare of thousands, and runs amuck in society as a wild beast that knows no mercy.

Such insane instincts, as a matter of fact, *do* exist among us, revealing their destructive ferocity in a thousand forms of sin and suffering.   Not a living soul has entirely escaped some injury, hereditary or immediate, direct or indirect, from their lordship.   Yet, we are instructed to regard them as scarcely modifiable factors of existence.   They recall to memory the fabulous monsters of ancient story, whose ravages were wont to carry terror to the hearts of men, until at length some hero went forth to slay them.   The monsters of to-day, unhappily, do not permit themselves to be slain so easily.   They spit fire as of yore ; they rend and pierce and tear ; but they are no longer to be overcome in one sharp struggle, after the fashion of their more worthy ancestors.

It is through the mysterious forces of heredity that the evil gathers such unholy strength.   It seems as if Nature had some mystic storehouse, wherein she garnered secretly, moment by moment, the thousand influences of daily life, the lurings and compulsions of circumstance ; and that these, accumulating silently, became transmuted into living passions, imperious needs, which we are wont to call "natural impulses," and to accept in the same resigned spirit as that in which the Germans welcome typhoid fever, as part of the Divine scheme. There is something appalling in the knowledge, that because a man's grandfather allowed evil habits to grow on him, that man is to be cursed all his life with some awful punishment; tormented, perhaps, with a strength of mere crude instinct entirely out of harmony with his real character, causing him infinite struggles, unless the worse thing happen— again through the existence of some hereditary weakness—and he surrenders the human side of him to the encroachments of the animal.

It is equally appalling to realise, that every man, woman, and child—stupid, weak, ignorant, as each may be—is busy forming the forces of heredity. It is not only parents of children who take part in this work ; parents of thoughts and of deeds are also called to "the making of the world."

Such facts, while adding to the sense of moral responsibility, must make clear the utter folly of accepting the leading characteristics of the average man of to-day as the final type of humanity.

We have seen how social conditions have given encouragement to primitive passions ; and it needs but little perspicacity to infer that the standard of what is a necessary indulgence of such passions, is likely to rise very high in these circumstances, just as a man's idea of the moderate and necessary amount of smoking or drinking rises with the facilities for gratifying these tastes. A fixed opinion gradually grows up that a man more or less *needs* these luxuries ; and universal custom has even gone the length of producing a strange idea among many, that their health demands the use of alcohol ; not as an occasional stimulus, but as a habitual prop to the system. Perhaps, after a time, they actually *do* arrive at such a morbid state (and this applies, of course, not merely to alcohol), for one of the insidious dangers of these superstitions is, that the artificially created needs become real ones after a while, constituting a sort of disease, which has to be propitiated by a form of food which exasperates the disease.

If we are to judge by results, we must surely conclude that habits have grown up in society, which are at least as pernicious as those of the victim of chloral or of opium. Doubtless, if it became general to indulge in these drugs, our standard of what was " necessary," or, at any rate, of what no man could be expected to do without, would rise to the level that now regulates the supply of these slaves of habit. Just as an individual can found a robust dynasty of tyrants in his body and his soul, so can an entire race enthral itself ; and in this case also, as in that of the individual, the demoniac possession will not be regarded as disease, but as a normal state, which indeed it is, but not the healthy or the necessary one.

When a man falls down in an epileptic fit, we conclude that he has something wrong with him. But if epileptic fits occurred by hundreds every day, and continued to do so persistently, the disease would soon cease to be regarded as a sign of anything abnormal. We might deplore the prevalence of epilepsy, but we should come to regard it as an accompaniment of life, and to smile at enthusiasts who supposed that society could exist without it.

" My dear sir," we should say, smoothing our moustaches, " when you come to have a little more experience of the world, you will understand that Human Nature is always Human Nature, and that fits are a natural concomitant of—er—civilised existence. I assure you, my father and grandfather used to go under the table with them every night. This, of course, is going rather to excess; I should be the last person to encourage immoderate indulgence, but I have no patience with your faddists who are always preaching self-restraint. If a man's fits don't go beyond his quiet six or seven a week, it doesn't do him a bit of harm. It's only when it comes on towards your fourteen or fifteen that it begins to knock a hole in his constitution."

We should thus learn to distinguish between the moderate man, and the reprobate who kept on having fits, in season and out of season. We should condemn, though in a more or less genial spirit, the jovial sinner who was a disgrace to the district, owing to the extraordinary frequency of his paroxysms. It was really becoming difficult to catch him in a lucid interval. Reformers would spring up to cope with the sad prevalence of the evil, whose consequences, in family life, would be the theme of many eloquent orations. For what sort of comfort and happiness could be expected in a domestic circle where the father of the family was perpetually falling down in convulsions, terrifying the children, scaring the neighbours, and letting loose in the peaceful precincts of home the avenging Phantom of an Epileptic Past ?

Something parallel to this has, in fact, happened with regard to some of the savageries that run riot amongst us. We see and regret their results, but we believe the evil to rest upon natural and necessary impulses which only dreamers can hope to see modified to any considerable extent. Such being our melancholy conviction, we feel it unavoidable to continue to offer as propitiation to the ravenous monster an entire sex, and so keep him in riotous health and spirits. As for our lop-sided attempts at restraint, the monster only regards them as affording him a little healthy exercise. He has all society for a happy hunting-ground.

If, then, we find that the ferocity of primitive impulses creates heart-breaking evils, can we hesitate in pronouncing these passions to have gone far beyond the limit of the necessary ? Have they not passed the limit of the endurable ? Can we fail to see, that their overindulgence has engendered in the race a morbid condition which may very well be compared to that of the opium-eater ? If it be true that a resolute rebellion against their tyranny brings punishment in its train, is not this exactly parallel to the vengeance taken on the slave of a nerve-destroying drug ? But even if this be denied (on the ground that the taking of drugs is not a natural but an acquired instinct), it can surely not be doubted that it would be possible to modify the force of the " oceanic brute," not merely by general cultivation of self-control (now a neglected department of education), but by the encouragement of desires which are more conducive to development and happiness.

The average man appears to be pitifully lacking in mental resource. If he has not something to destroy, Time is his enemy. If in this frame of mind, his forms of amusement are not more or less brutalising, he has not the wisdom of Society to thank. Her methods are all coercive rather than educating. Yet, we recognise that the teacher who seeks to touch the mind and soul by attacking the body, belongs to the Dark Ages. We are beginning to understand, that we can only eradicate a habit or weaken an instinct, by altering the processes of the intellect, of the conscience, of the will, and, finally, of the physical constitution. The enemy has to be met and fought within the man's own soul, not merely by laws from without. The real triumph is to destroy the tendency to evil, or the desire to practise at the expense of others what might, in itself, be innocent.

We can only teach to any purpose when we have made the pupil willing to learn. And to this end, his circumstances must conspire.

There are in man many regions of the conscience as well as of the intellect still uncultivated. The elements of existence have to be remodelled in order to redeem these wastes. But to deny the possibility of redemption is to ignore the testimony of all history.

The very fact that our conditions are so preposterous, so ruinous to all chance of a healthy moral life, is a ground for entertaining high hopes of human possibilities, when these conditions shall be more propitious.

"There are," says Maudesley, "many inconsistencies of thought and character which might . . . be brought forward to show how far men yet are from doing justice to their mental faculties by developing them consistently to the utmost of their capacities."

It is not beyond human power, though it may, in its first steps, be terribly difficult, to destroy the barbarous survivals that now desecrate the relations of the sexes. But that accomplished, even partially—through the might of growing opinion—a universal change of standard would become inevitable.

Imagine a troop of schoolboys with a cageful of birds at their mercy. What sort of views would be likely to grow up amongst the boys as to their right to amuse themselves at the expense of the prisoners? Moral precepts would be in vain so long as the birds remained behind the bars. But release the captives, and the owners, perforce, cease their tyranny. In a short time, their conscience harmonises with the changed conditions, and virtue soon begins to be manufactured out of necessity.

A change of opinion is confusedly arising, even among the majority, who insist that no alteration of sentiment is called for. They wear their rue with a difference.

Just as people will read fresh meanings into old religious doctrines, so there is a strong tendency to take a new view of human relations. In opposition to this more civilised feeling, many still point back to what are called the "facts" of social existence. The origin of those facts we shall find in man's absolute power over woman, and in the inevitable abuse of that power, to his own and her age-long injury. " Practical " philosophy preached, and still preaches, the absolute necessity of these depredations, and the belief (otherwise expressed) became firmly fixed : that the nature of man demands the martyrdom of woman.

Thus we find the foundation of our great twin-system of marriage and prostitution.

It is often regarded as unfair to treat men as the only offenders ; women, it is urged, are not so often sinned against as sinning, and they are generally the first to point out to men the descent to Avernus.   This may be true or false ; probably it is partly true, for the mere fact of womanhood does not provide an antidote against the moral poison that is generated by evil lives and evil thoughts.   Men hand on their weaknesses to their daughters as well as to their sons, and cruel is often the suffering caused by such a heritage, under the conditions of a woman's life.

It is the system rather than the sex that deserves reproach.

If the fault is really to be laid at the door of women, then it is because of the training they have received at the hands of their fellows.   Their field of life having been ruthlessly curtailed, we must not be surprised if we find them trying to make the most of what is vouchsafed to them, and practising the only permitted arts in a somewhat destructive fashion.   In short, whichever may be the peccant sex, or whether or not both are equally culpable, the fact remains that the real first cause of the corruption is the *position that one holds in respect to the other.*   To bicker over minor causes, to seek to weigh out blame with nicety, is merely to confuse the mind in the mazes of these intricate problems.   Heap upon women all the reproach and leave men spotless, if so it be desired—the conclusion remains steady and unaltered: that men's rule and women's subjection lie at the root of all the evil and distress.   That such results would follow from such antecedents might have been predicted *a priori ;* we have long and painful experience to confirm such a process of reasoning.

Whatever may be thought as to the amount of blame attaching to women in these matters, it is, however, generally the nature of *men* that is indulgently considered, when there is a question of methods of reform.   Women may be regarded as sinful,and as leading others in the paths of sin, but we hear nothing about the demands of *their* nature, which makes transgression necessary or change impracticable.   Whence this distinction may be gathered: that a man's delinquencies are required by his " nature "; a woman's, detestable aberrations to be punished with all the scorn and ferocity of an outraged society.   Yet, if women are equal to men in iniquity, how does it happen that they, too, have not imperious " natures " that must be indulged at all hazards ?

We can scarcely fail to see the absurdity of assuming a certain state of the human constitution to be the result of an eternal law, when all evidence points to that state as the result of man's own accumulated habits, by which he has been reduced to slavery.   Probably, this slavery is often endured because the man has been persistently trained to think submission inevitable.   There is no enemy so awe-inspiring as one's own despair of victory.

If we are really to take human nature exactly as we find it, and provide respectfully for its manifold demands, heaven help our descendants !   The imperious natures of our grandfathers called out for wine in such liberal quantities that they ended their repasts under the table. Thence the imperious nature of our gout.   What is often called common-sense is opposed to revolutions, even when directed against the tyranny of evil habits.   When such habits engender rheumatism and consumption and heart-disease, the sufferers have to bear their pains, for they have not yet found the means to thrust these penalties directly on to other shoulders (vivisection seeks to accomplish this indirectly). But when the folly and wickedness that circulate in the blood break forth, in the form of fierce passions ; then their force may be expended to the injury of other human beings, who are plentifully provided by the foresight of society, as its scapegoats. All pain and trouble thus are spared—for the moment—to the heir of the ages. He settles his account later on.

It may take some time yet, before mankind arrives at the point of understanding the meanness of thus thrusting suffering on others which fate has apportioned for oneself. An age which sees nothing dastardly in the practice of torturing animals in the supposed interests of mankind, is not in a condition to see that it is carrying out the same cowardly principle as regards certain doomed classes of humanity. Lecky speaks of the unhappy woman of whom the " respectable " think with an undisguised shudder, as " the most efficient guardian of virtue. She remains, while creeds and civilisations rise and fall, the eternal priestess of humanity, blasted for the sins of the people."

PART IV

THE HUMAN ELEMENT IN MAN

*" The Word is well said to be omnipotent in this world, man, thereby divine,
can create as by a fiat."*—CARLYLE.

THE human race has arrived at a point in its development,
when the disturbance consequent upon its transitional
condition begins to be severely felt. The inharmony between our civilisation and our still unconquered barbarism,
becomes intolerable ; and there is an outcry—not against
the barbarism, but against the civilisation. Men blame
the civilised state for the evil that is caused therein by
the savageries which they have failed to extirpate ; and
a cry is raised for a return to Nature. And Nature [1] is
always waiting eagerly, like a hungry beast of prey, to
reclaim her own. She rejoices at the falling to pieces of
the State which had defied her incessant endeavour to
undo it ; in the voluntary surrender to the crude impulses
which have always held the civilised in a state of siege.

She triumphs in the stupendous waste of power and
effort implied in this retracing of the steep uphill road
that has been trodden by so many weary feet, for so
many troublous centuries. The fruitless agony and toil
of Sisyphus, who has to watch the huge stone that he has
so painfully thrust to the summit of the hill, blundering
stupidly down again to the lowest point that its idiot
weight unswervingly suggests : this is a sight after
Nature's own heart.

In the progress from stage to stage of life, there come
inevitable epochs of confusion and darkness. Who does
not know that the paths of development are full of

---

[1] Nature is here used in its usual popular sense of primitive impulse
and law, unmodified by human intelligence or moral development.

shadowed places? Man is naturally impatient of such obscurity. He hates to grope. He prefers to turn his steps backwards. He indolently justifies the cruelties of life,—the torture of the weak by the strong, the rule of man over woman, the oppression of animals by mankind,—by the authority of Nature. It does not disturb him that the existence of the State, as such, depends upon a *departure* from Nature. Throughout the universe, he urges, the same eternal law holds sway; let not the weak, above all let not woman, seek to evade it. But that is exactly what every progressive being *has* to do, if he wishes to avoid degeneration. That is what the merest vegetable has to do, if it is to escape the atavism that sets in as soon as it has to resign itself to natural processes. All its complexities of structure, the glorifications of its original forms and organs, disappear, and it reverts to a weedy, undeveloped growth, struggling for standing room, with a host of unkempt brothers in adversity. Nature has no mercy on those who yield themselves to her dominion. She bids the very flowers of the field bring forth millions of seeds, that one may survive; she raises myriads of strong young lives, where there is no possibility of their continuance; lives of plants, lives of men—it is all one—full of yearning and the mysterious "will to live," yet foredoomed to slow processes of decay.

In opposition to the widely-accepted theory that whatever is natural is always right, it would be almost safe to assert, that whatever is natural is certain to be wrong. It is unquestionably by becoming less and less "natural" that the human being becomes more and more tolerable. It is by presenting to the imagination, a new method of diverging from the tame and barren wastes of "Nature" unredeemed, that a new step of progress is begun.

There has been a very strong tendency, of late, to an entirely opposite view, although those who hold it do not make even an attempt at consistency; for they profess no belief, after all, that society ought to return to entirely natural conditions, which would commend the adventurous highwayman and the sturdy housebreaker to the support of a wise government.

There are, however, some who go even to this length: holding that we suffer from over-civilisation, and that it is folly to protect the weak against the strong, since this policy confuses natural selection and enfeebles the race. They are prepared to defy the fact, that in a community where each man had to be perpetually on the defensive, he would have leisure for very little else, so that art and industry must languish. Then, " Nature " would have a gala time of it !

The intelligent mechanic, whose conversation with her father Emma Hooker Woodward records, perceived plainly how entirely artificial was the condition induced by education in any form, for when asked why he opposed " the Act that brought it within reach of the poorest," his answer was : " I go agin it on principle, Sir, not because of its unconstitutionality, but because it's onnat'ral. Ign'rance is nat'ral," he said. " We was born ign'rant and ought to be kep' so." The intelligent mechanic was only more logical and dauntless, in his application of the principle, than others who hold the same creed.

Either, then, we must take primitive nature for our guide, or we must choose a gentler sovereign. In the second case, we should obey Nature only when her crude compulsion proved too strong for the resistance of weaklings, enervated by the centuries of obedience which our ancestors have devoted to the barbaric goddess. In defying her power, on the other hand, we should make progress in the *human* direction, adding in some sort to the creation, as an artist adds to it, who brings form and being out of inchoate material.

There is no question more difficult for man to answer

P

than " What is good ? " or " What is evil ? " It is utterly
false to assert that every man knows in his heart, in
each case, the right from the wrong.

At critical moments, the power of early training and
the prejudices of his race, assert themselves as oracles,
unless their exact opposites have usurped their functions,
through a violent reaction. But if, in particular cases,
the decision be difficult, there is a general analogy
between what we may call good and that which is, in its
essence, organising or creative. Order, balance, form,
method, life : these, in the sentient world, are beneficent :
while disorder, aimlessness, formlessness, disruptiveness,
incoherence, death, stand on the other side as evil. Now
nature—in the sense of primitive impetus—is the high
priestess of all that is fortuitous and incoherent.

Imagine, for a moment, the career of one who really
allowed her guidance, unresisted. And imagine the still
more appalling fate of a whole society which accepted
her counsels without question. In such a case—almost
inconceivable—the man and the race must instantly
undergo a process of disintegration, till reduced to their
original raw material. They would suffer the moral
death which they courted.

Of course " good " and " evil " are terms relative to
human consciousness. The race progresses in its conception of good. In a healthy state, the creative forces
are ever busily at work. They form, and fashion, and
sustain, showing a marked contrast to the decadent
condition, when everything grows slack, falls apart, slips
back towards chaos.

If a man is to extend the limits of his universe, he
has to build up a larger and more *creative* consciousness.
This can certainly never be done under the guidance of
primitive natural impulses. Man has to escape from
the vicious circle of these, or to remain a prisoner, for
ever, in a narrow dungeon.

An image of an ideal human soul might perhaps be

found in that masterpiece of ancient art, the Pantheon, whose serene magnificence inspires while it soothes the imagination. Its vastness is filled with infinite richness of subordinate beauty, sustaining without disturbing the splendour of the great temple, through whose stupendous and shadowy dome, the blue of heaven is seen by day, and, at night, the stars look down.

Life may be to a man a temple of this magnificence or the most wretched of hovels, exactly as he permits the enslaving or the liberative forces of his being to obtain the mastery. Our present life, in the heart of civilisation, is a fierce struggle between these elements ; between the original idiotcy of savage appetite, and the acquired wisdom of less material aspiration. We of the nineteenth century, are at once too civilised and too barbarous to rest content with the half animal, half human standards that form our social organisation. The human in us is strong enough to be wounded and outraged by the barbarity wherein we are still plunged ; but we are not sufficiently human, as yet, to insist on the extirpation of that savage basis to our existence. Not a breath is drawn by the noblest of the race, which is not drawn involuntarily at the expense of pain or sacrifice to some other being. It is scarcely possible for any one to escape this curse which rests upon the human family. Were we more wholly savage, we should feel no pain in these conditions. The beast of prey probably finds life very satisfactory. He is not tormented by the thousand incongruities, inequalities of development in the individual nature, and in that of the race, which disturb so cruelly the life of the civilised. The more we develop, the more keen will be the anguish that we shall suffer from these survivals, but the more broad and exquisite our power of enjoyment. All change in the direction of greater complexity has, seemingly, to be accomplished through bitter struggle, and often through sin and failure and humiliation. This conflict is the secret of half the pain of life.

Thus, in an age called materialistic, we are forced
back with stronger impulsion than ever to believe or
to hope in some power that is formative and coherent,
beyond and in man's own soul (or whatever we may
choose to call that which we all more or less imply by
the latter word).   This " soul " gives to man the only
hold which he has over the formation of his conditions,
and the only means of influencing his fate.   Through
the working of Thought and the masonry of Will, the
whole fabric of life is rebuilt.   Creed and usage are
transmuted, atom by atom.   An idea is a soul that
creates for itself a body, and that body may eventually
swell into a new social order, nay, into a new world !

Thus considered, Nature does not stand apart from
man, for man—aspiring, progressive, victorious over
primal impulse—is still a part of Nature, and obedient,
in a higher sense, to her dictates than he ever was in
the infancy of the race.

So that if we regard Nature in this wider sense: as
including all that the universe contains, or all that the
powers of man can ultimately perceive or command, he
is not in real revolt against her when he ceases to be a
half-redeemed savage.   Nature will not, in the long run,
punish him for such emancipation of the god within
him, from the idiot, who has carried on for so many ages
his senseless rule.   She will acknowledge and bow to
the divinity.

She has shown her approbation of man's progress in
a thousand ways, and in ways most unexpected.   The
man who is the outcome of civilisation, with all the evil
conditions that he has therein to contend with, with all
the thousand foes to health that surround him in the
restless life of modern communities, that man is yet
stronger, physically, than the savage who has lived what
we call a natural life from his infancy, and has a long
line of ancestors who so lived, behind him.   The nervous
force in the savage, while it has endured fewer shocks,

has received less cultivation. It is in nervous organisation that the civilised are more complex, more highly wrought, more lords of themselves. Thus, while the latter are, it would seem, incomparably more capable of pain than are their untutored brothers (who undergo ordeals that would be torture to ourselves with scarcely a sign or a groan), yet, if it be a question of endurance of hardship over a long period, when courage of what may be called the nervous kind is required, then the civilised man lasts out where the savage succumbs almost immediately. His actual physical strength is less than that of the civilised, in such conditions. He seems to stand to the educated, more complex example of the race, as a straggling weed stands to a cultivated plant, whose qualities have been improved by intelligence and art.

Civilised man suffers indeed from his own follies; from the persistence with which he lives, and forces others to live, in circumstances which every handbook of medical science assures him are inimical to body and mind ; yet, with all those easily removable disadvantages, the general education of nerve and mind that he has received, has ended by producing a more physically efficient human being, who has *not* been made to pay for spiritual advance by bodily degeneration. It is not spiritual advance, but spiritual blindness that he has had to pay for. It is a fact full of hope and significance, that sane, steady mental activity of any kind, so long as it be not carried on under conditions of anxiety, or pushed to wild excess, has a life-giving effect upon the body, tending to the balance and regulation of all its forces.

All this tends to show that the dictates of primitive nature are not, by any means, the best guides to physical well-being. And if this may be said of the savage whose surroundings are in harmony with such promptings, how much more must it be said of the civilised man, whose conditions clash so perilously with the non-social passions? Can one not foresee possibilities of human development beyond anything that has hitherto been dreamt of by man? Instead of physical degeneration, in consequence of the more highly organised life, is there not every promise of indefinite improvement, even in physical powers, probably in length of life and in prolongation of youth? These things follow if the others be true. It may appear Utopian to expect so much, but so would have seemed a prophecy of the conditions of our present state (with all its troubles) to the most hopeful of our ancestors.

As for the change being impracticable, changes have always been impracticable until they took place. Let not *that* dismay us !

It will be said that such standards, in hopeless opposition to the strongest impulses of the race, are absolutely useless when we have to deal with complex social problems. Human nature, as it now is fashioned (through whatever causes), is too fierce an animal to be tamed thus by means of transcendental principles. A man cares not how he came by his passions, all he wants is to gratify them.

But this is not true. It is the perennial mistake of what we call the practical mind. History is a tissue of transcendental principles solidified into national religions, aspirations, policies, laws, conventions, revolutions. From the day when human beings formed into communities, they began to fashion for themselves standards which referred them to some object more or less raised above that of mere selfishness. The idea of the tribe gave a stimulus to sentiment not self-directed. From the beginning, it is almost safe to say, there has been a religious element in human society, different from that mere terror, or desire to propitiate an unseen foe—generally at the expense of some weaker brother—which is so often called by that name.

And it is a striking fact, that for the sake of this religion, men have shown themselves able to defy the most powerful instincts of their nature.

There is no "normal" propensity that is really beyond control, even in the present excited condition of human propensities, with all heredity and all circumstance at their back. The authority has only to be strong enough, and mankind desires nothing better than to obey. At the command of one man, perhaps dead centuries since, whole nations order their lives. Some prophet, whose very existence is so enveloped in clouds of legend and fable, that the man himself seems scarcely more than a fable, can hold in thrall vast lands and populations, century after century ; promise, threaten, command ; dictate beliefs, actions, abstentions, to millions of his fellows. At his voice, calling for ever across the ages, "natural instincts" crouch down in submission, and passions subside—the animal is conquered, and the man is born.

Once more, mankind is *not* the slave of primitive instinct, except when mankind so wills it. It is not instinct but emotional belief that has moved the world. Instinct has troubled, harassed, and often unfashioned that which human faith and mind and sympathy have built up, but it has not played the leading part, or we should not now be in a position even to discuss the matter. We should all be scalping our enemies round some forest fire, and employing what faint glimmers of intelligence we possessed to add to the extremity of their tortures.

The world is ruled through the creeds of mankind ; and those creeds are woven, strand after strand, by the ceaseless efforts of individuals, most of whom are unconscious that they are thus plying the immortal business of the Fates.

THE END

Lightning Source UK Ltd.
Milton Keynes UK
UKOW051915310112

186386UK00001BA/1/P